AFTERLIFE

The Complete Guide to Life after Death

CAROL NEIMAN & EMILY GOLDMAN

VIKING
STUDIO
BOOKS

A LABYRINTH BOOK

VIKING STUDIO BOOKS
Published by the Penguin Group
Penguin Books USA Inc., 375 Hudson Street, New York, New York 10014, U.S.A.
Penguin Books Ltd, 27 Wrights Lane, London, W8 5TZ, England
Penguin Books Australia Ltd, Ringwood, Victoria, Australia
Penguin Books Canada Ltd, 10 Alcorn Avenue, Toronto, Ontario, Canada M4V 3B2
Penguin Books (N.Z.) Ltd, 182-190 Wairau Road, Auckland 10, New Zealand

Penguin Books Ltd, Registered Offices:
Harmondsworth, Middlesex, England.

First American edition
Published in 1994 by Viking Penguin, a division of Penguin Books USA Inc.

1 3 5 7 9 10 8 6 4 2

Copyright © Labyrinth Publishing (UK) Ltd., 1994
All rights reserved

First published in Great Britain by Boxtree Ltd.

Produced by Labyrinth Publishing (UK) Ltd.

LIBRARY OF CONGRESS CATALOGING-IN-PUBLICATION DATA
Neiman, Carol and Goldman, Emily.
Afterlife: the complete guide to life after death / by Emily Goldman
p. cm.
ISBN 0-670-85732-7
1. Future life. 2. Spiritualism. 3. ghosts. I Title.
BL 535. G65 1994
291.2'3—dc20   94-9625

Printed in Singapore
Set by Carmen Strider
Designed by Carmen Strider

CONTENTS

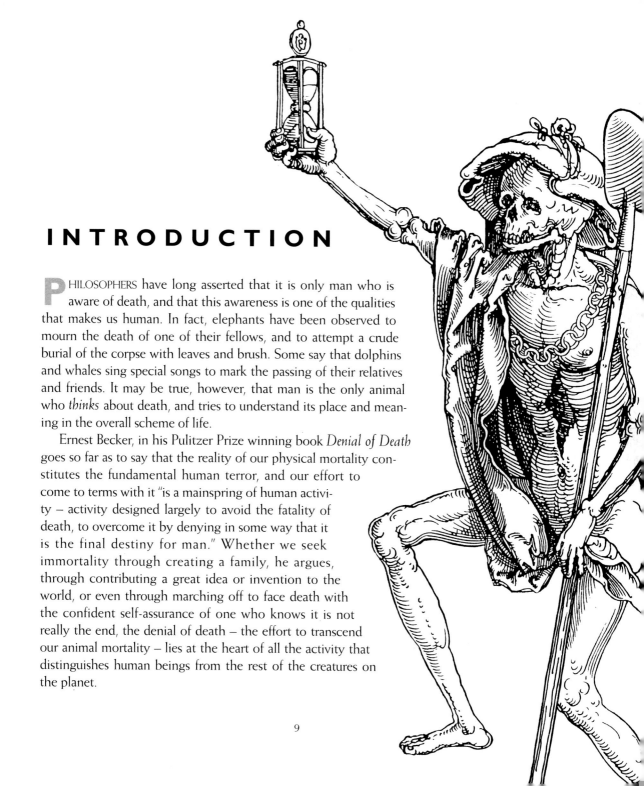

INTRODUCTION

PHILOSOPHERS have long asserted that it is only man who is aware of death, and that this awareness is one of the qualities that makes us human. In fact, elephants have been observed to mourn the death of one of their fellows, and to attempt a crude burial of the corpse with leaves and brush. Some say that dolphins and whales sing special songs to mark the passing of their relatives and friends. It may be true, however, that man is the only animal who *thinks* about death, and tries to understand its place and meaning in the overall scheme of life.

Ernest Becker, in his Pulitzer Prize winning book *Denial of Death* goes so far as to say that the reality of our physical mortality constitutes the fundamental human terror, and our effort to come to terms with it "is a mainspring of human activity – activity designed largely to avoid the fatality of death, to overcome it by denying in some way that it is the final destiny for man." Whether we seek immortality through creating a family, he argues, through contributing a great idea or invention to the world, or even through marching off to face death with the confident self-assurance of one who knows it is not really the end, the denial of death – the effort to transcend our animal mortality – lies at the heart of all the activity that distinguishes human beings from the rest of the creatures on the planet.

9

Despite the lack of empirical evidence of life beyond death, most cultures have developed elaborate visions of what awaits them in the hereafter.

Most of us, as Becker and many other philosophers have pointed out, rarely allow the full impact of the paradox of being human to surface. Paradoxes are troublesome, even agonizing, and the paradox of being human perhaps the most agonizing of all. To quote Becker again: "Man is literally split in two: he has an awareness of his own splendid uniqueness in that he sticks out of nature with a towering majesty, and yet he goes back into the ground a few feet in order blindly and dumbly to rot and disappear forever." So we bury the truth of this human dilemma in our everyday lives – usually with some success – until someone close to us dies, or until our own bodies begin to show symptoms of old age and decrepitude. Then the whole thorny question forces its way to the surface and, if we are very alert, we might realize it has been subtly harrassing us and determining our actions and beliefs all the time, even when we weren't looking.

It is impossible that anything so natural, so necessary, and so universal as death, should ever have been designed by Providence as an evil to mankind.
Jonathan Swift (1667-1745) *Thoughts on Religion*

The attitude of acceptance that underlies these words of Jonathan Swift is so matter-of-fact, so logical, and so comforting that it is almost a surprise that not everyone shares it. But while this attitude might be logical, the logic of the mind does little to console the deeper terrors of the heart. Fears of suffering and annihilation have plagued humankind from its very beginnings, and continue to plague the elemental and "primitive" man or woman within us all. Deep down, in that place Jung has defined as the collective unconscious, we all know that the dark is scary and wild animals can come along and rip us to pieces. Death may be "natural" but Nature is not always nice.

Death may be necessary, too, but the life force within us is stubbornly reluctant to throw in the towel without a fight. Whether it is Dylan Thomas raging against the dying of the light, or Lucian's array of characters trying to strike bargains with Death's ferryman Charon, most of us would just as soon decline the invitation, thank you very much. Maybe, in postponing the inevitable, we can find the time to get used to the idea. Or, even better, come to know just exactly what we are getting into when we enter that ferryboat to make the journey to the other shore.

*20th-century medicine has made it possible for more
and more people to be revived from clinical "death."
Their experiences are provoking us to take a look at
a subject we have avoided for centuries.*

As the Persian proverb, and countless similar proverbs remind us, "Death is a camel that lies down at every door." We may try to take issue with its naturalness or its necessity, but the universality of death mocks our efforts at every turn. This fact of death lurks at the heart of every spiritual search, and indeed, as many astute observers of human behavior have pointed out, religion would probably not be necessary without it. Strip down the doctrines of any of the world's major religions, and at the core you will find a preoccupation with what happened before, and what happens after, the life that we can all observe and participate in here on earth. Even the instructions for living in the "here" are for the most part inextricably bound up with events in the "after," whether that "after" is Christianity's Judgment Day, or Hinduism's rebirth into another "here."

While it is true that many of the ancient Greeks – and the Jews up until about the second century BC – seem to have held the view that death was pretty much the end, and the "afterlife" just a sort of half-conscious shadow existence, this idea has never inspired the development of a widely popular religion. Although contemporary humankind might have drawn nearer to the opinion of Seneca that heaven was invented by the ambitious, hell was invented by rogues, and only fools believed in either of them, we would still like to think that there is *something* out there *somewhere* after we die. The hardcore materialism expressed by philosophers like Pascal – who suggested that 'The last act is tragic, however happy all the rest of the play is; at the last a little earth is thrown upon our head, and that is the end for ever"[1] – seems to imply an ultimate meaninglessness that is simply too hard for most of us to take.

Fortunately, men and women have appeared throughout the ages who have been able to look us in the eye with a straight face and tell us that we are more than just matter, and that our consciousness consists of more than just an accidental combination of chemicals and processes confined to a mass of stuff encased in our skulls. "No man ever spoke thus," it was said of Jesus, and when he spoke of the Kingdom of God there was something in the unwavering directness of his gaze, in the aura of peace and love that surrounded his person, that persuaded those around him that he knew what he was talking about.

The problem, however, is that the expression of great spiritual truths is notoriously difficult, and those who have had direct personal access to the experiences upon which these truths are

*Dante Alighieri's Divine Comedy consolidated the
medieval Christian view of the hereafter and
planted it firmly in the minds of Christians for
generations to come.*

based have been notoriously few. A Jesus might know from his own experience that he is "with God" and that we all have the same potential, but we find it so hard to comprehend the full meaning of what he says that we can only "believe" what he says is true. This belief becomes a substitute for the direct "knowing" that gave rise to what Jesus said in the first place. And as time passes, the belief system surrounding him is elaborated more and more by those who are farther and farther removed from the essential, nonverbal ingredients of his message – in other words, from the alive "presence" who convinced us that what he was saying must be true.

It is impossible to know what Jesus himself would say about the church that was eventually created around him, but it seems unlikely that the gentle man from Bethlehem would have approved of some of the wars and persecutions that have been carried out in his name. Similar questions could be raised about all the world's major religions: would their founders really approve of the current interpretations of what they said in their lifetimes, or the dogmas that have been elaborated around their teachings? They themselves may have resolved the fundamental human paradox, may have reached an understanding of the essential unity of the material and spiritual nature of man, but their followers have exhibited an unfortunate tendency to remain stuck in the struggle with the apparent duality of these two sides of the human condition.

Nowhere has this struggle been more evident than in the construction of beliefs about the afterlife. Layer upon layer of otherworldly paradises and hells have been created, refined, re-evaluated and recreated over the centuries, along with the ways and means to get to the good places and avoid the bad ones. Words that might have been originally intended to be allegory and indication towards a spiritual condition have become the pegs upon which to hang specific and decidedly material realities: hell became literally a place of fire and brimstone, heaven a physical place somewhere above the clouds.

These notions have taken a quite a beating in the scientific age, of course, and few people really believe in them anymore. Nowadays, in a world where only a fraction of people in the post-industrial Western countries bother to make even an occasional visit to a church or synagogue, we have invented new and more up-to-date hereafters. There are alien "walk-ins" among us, we are told, who have taken over the bodies of willing spirits at the intersection between life and death. They then come back, in their newly acquired disguise, to prepare us for a cataclysmic millennial upheaval. Some even hint that these aliens, and the mysterious lights in the sky that herald their coming, intend to choose some of us to be saved and "re-seeded" onto the planet once the 21st-century apocalyptic dust has settled. Others, putting more faith in the science of earthlings than in that of the extraterrestrials, have decided to have themselves deep-frozen at death in the hope that somebody, sometime, will not only find a cure for their deceased condition, but be interested in bringing them back when they do.

Nobody knows, in fact, what death is, nor whether to man
it is not perchance the greatest of all blessings; yet people fear it as if they surely knew it to be the
worst of evils.
Socrates, in Plato's *Apology*

In recent decades, earthly science has brought an unprecedented opportunity for thousands of ordinary people who in previous times would have taken a one-way journey into death to make a return trip and tell us what it was like. Many of them have come back with wondrous and moving stories of their experience that suggest that perchance death is indeed "the greatest of all blessings," and certainly nothing to fear. Some tell stories of traveling to luminous worlds where they are greeted by loving beings. Others tell of panoramic visions of the events in their lives that amount to a kind of intimate, personal, and utterly non-judgmental review of both good deeds accomplished and hurtful acts inflicted on others. An extraordinary number of those who have passed through this "life review" assert that they now understand that love is the most important quality to cultivate in our lives. Almost all of them speak of a blissful detachment from the body during their experiences, and many report that they have felt quite free from their usual emotional entanglements as well.

When they are told they must return to life, these travelers to the borders of the hereafter often obey reluctantly. But once they are back they find an appreciation for the beauty of life that they have never experienced before. They are no longer afraid of death, they say, because now they know that death is not the end. And, true to the promise of the sages, many of them attest that this knowledge has transformed their lives in the herenow, as if they have awakened from a long sleep.

their underlying assumptions as faulty and get on with our business. That business, after a preliminary review of our inherited notions of the hereafter, will be to look at what the near-death experience might tell us today about another reality, normally hidden from us but as universal, natural, and perhaps even necessary as death itself.

We are left with the nagging question of how actual *dead* people experience the hereafter – or indeed, if there is such a thing that we would recognize as "experience" there at all. In fact, the Eastern wisdom traditions have some opinions to offer, and these will also be examined. In addition, we will dip into a smattering of evidence that there is indeed something like an afterlife, as it can be gathered from sightings of ghosts and apparitions. And we will acknowledge the phenomenon of spirits who have spoken or otherwise demonstrated their presence with the help of living "mediums," and offer some advice to those who might choose to make their own connections with those who have "gone beyond" in this particular way.

In the end, it is my feeling – and in fact most of the wisdom traditions stress this fact at the same time they are trying to offer some clues to the answer – that the question of what happens *after* death, and not simply "near" it, must remain a mystery until the time comes for us to experience it for ourselves.

For that ultimate journey, it will be good to keep in mind some advice from the Native American culture, advice that still contains the memory of a time untainted by either scientific prejudices or the orthodox religious doctrines of the so-called civilized world. Death, they say, is an event "as intimate between the individual and the Earth Mother as the moment of birth is between human mother and child." Some things, and perhaps the most precious things, can only be experienced within the inarticulate depths of the spirit. And finally, they say, "When it is your time to pass, it should be with your mind wide open and your prayer in your heart."   *Carol Neiman*

In the traditions of Native Americans and many other tribal peoples, the world of spirit and the manifest world are not so distinctly separate as they are in more recently developed cultures. The spirits of the dead simply take their place in a natural world already filled with spirits, and under the proper circumstances are available to give advice and counsel to the living.

THE NATIVE AMERICAN WAY OF DEATH

In the old way, when it was time to die, old ones would go off by themselves, feeling that the moment of death was as intimate between them and the Earth Mother as the moment of birth is between human mother and child. They would find a quiet place and there make prayers to the Great Spirit, thanking him for the life they had enjoyed. They would sing their song, and they would die.

There is a story of one old-timer who felt his time had come. He invited all of his friends to a gathering where they sang songs and made a feast. He had a big give-away, giving gifts to all his friends, telling them how happy he had been with their friendship. They, in turn, all spoke their good thoughts of him. Then, while they were singing songs, he closed his eyes and died. Many Indian people have been known to predict the exact date and time they would die.

Warrior societies used to let the old men go into battle one last time. When they went, the young men would stand aside and say, "Let the old man count one last coup."

Another Indian custom was to give away or make arrangements to give away everything a person had before he died. That way there was nothing for anyone to fight over after the person was gone.

Like all other things in life, death is not permanent. It is but a change from one world, from one state of being into another. For those of us who learn to love life, with all of its changes, death should not be a fearful event. It should be a time of celebrating the continual evolution of the soul. When it is your time to pass, it should be with your mind wide open and your prayer in your heart. When one dear to you dies, besides sadness at your loss you should feel happiness that now the soul is free to soar to Kitche Manitou, the Great Spirit, our common Creator. Where there is love, there is no room for fear.

Sun Bear, from *Wild Fire* magazine

1

HIGHWAYS TO HEAVEN
ROADS TO HELL

They have no wool cloth, nor linen, nor cotton,
because they do not need any. Also they have no private
goods; all things are in common.
They live together without King, without Emperor,
and each one is Lord of himself....
Beyond that, they have no churches and keep no law,
and yet they are not idolatrous.
What shall I say,
except they live according to nature?

"Amerigo Vespucci," in Thomas More's *Utopia*

REMEMBRANCE OF THE HEREBEFORE

Details of a Chinese woodcut depicting the
"realm of the gods."

EACH LIFE begins with duality – the meeting of man and woman, sperm and egg, which in turn provokes the first division of the egg cell into two. This duality pursues us all our lives – "I" and "thou," right brain and left brain, heart and mind, earth and sky, heaven and hell...life and death. Even in the East, where the yin-yang symbol was invented to encompass these opposites and make them whole, the religious and philosophical tendency has been to choose the "thanatos" side of the coin over the "eros." Life on earth is perceived as a burden to be transcended in most Eastern religions, and a preference for the spiritual is implied in the mystic traditions of the West as well. With the coin of life in our hands, we seem to find it impossible to see both sides of it at once.

The catch is, of course, that as long as we are alive, the only side of the coin that is known to us for certain is the living, breathing, concrete, physical, material side. We can't *really* know what the other side looks like, or indeed even if the coin has another side, until we turn it over. All we can do is watch as our friends and relatives get ripped apart by wild animals and notice that afterwards, they aren't around any more – at least in a form that we can recognize and fit into its proper place on the face of any coin we can catch hold of.

*Most of the founders of the world's major religions
are endowed with the capacity to move
easily between the earthly and heavenly realms,
as Mohammed does in this painting.*

But at the same time, something tells us it was not always so. The same collective unconscious that remembers fearful nights and being ripped apart by wild animals also remembers a Golden Age which, in the words of Ovid, was "blessed with the fruit of trees and the herbs which the soil brings forth, and it did not pollute its mouth with gore. Then the birds in safety winged their way through the air and the hare fearlessly wandered through the fields, nor was the fish caught through its witlessness. There were no snares, and none feared treachery, but all was full of peace."[1] The biblical story of Eden paints essentially the same picture, as do Paradise myths all over the world.

"There were no gods in the Krita Yuga [Age of Truth, or the First Age]," says the *Mahabharata* of India's Hindus, "and there were no demons. The Krita Yuga was without disease; there was no lessening with the years; there was no hatred, or vanity, or evil thought whatsoever; no sorrow, no fear. In those times, men lived as long as they chose to live, and were without any fear of death."

And, according to the Chinese sage Chuang Tzu, "In the Age of Perfect Virtue they were upright and correct, without knowing that to be so was righteousness; they loved one another, without knowing that to do so was benevolence; they were honest and wholehearted without knowing that it was good faith; in their simple movements they employed the services of one another without thinking that they were conferring or receiving any gift. Therefore their actions left no track, and there was no record of their affairs."[2]

"There was a time when meadow, grove and stream," says Wordsworth, "did seem appareled in celestial light."[3] Somehow, from somewhere, we all seem to share this memory of paradise, this "herebefore" that is the ground and source of our being. The mystics tell us that this paradise is accessible here and now, that it is here that we find our true immortality and wear the face that we had before our parents were born. "What is the essence of your teaching?" the Zen master is asked, and his response is, simply, "This."

We listen to the words of the mystics, the beautiful stories of a paradise lost, and in those moments when we are not too preoccupied with our everyday affairs we often get the uncanny feeling that the words are not only true but express something we have always known. And it is upon this feeling of remembrance that we build our brightest hopes for the "hereafter," in the fragile but persistent hope that we can some day return to our lost home.

There was a time
when meadow, grove, and stream,
The earth, and every common sight,
To me did seem
Appareled in celestial light,
The glory and the freshness of a dream.
It is not now as it hath been of yore; –
Turn wheresoe'er I may,
By night or day,
The things which I have seen
I now can see no more...

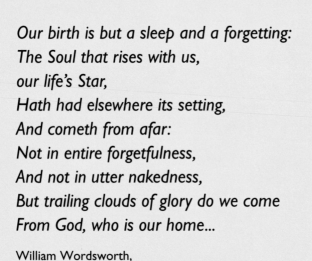

Our birth is but a sleep and a forgetting:
The Soul that rises with us,
our life's Star,
Hath had elsewhere its setting,
And cometh from afar:
Not in entire forgetfulness,
And not in utter nakedness,
But trailing clouds of glory do we come
From God, who is our home...

William Wordsworth,
Intimations of Immortality from Recollections of Early Childhood

"This is more or less what I would do if I had the power to dream every night of anything I wanted. Some months I would probably fulfill all the more obvious wishes. There might be palaces and banquets, players and dancing girls, fabulous bouts of love, and sunlit gardens beside lakes, with mountains beyond. There would next be long conversations with sages, contemplation of supreme works of art, hearing and playing music, voyages to foreign lands, flying out into space to see the galaxies, and delving into the atom to watch the wiggling wavicles. But the night would come when I might want to add a little spice of adventure - perhaps a dream of dangerous mountain climbing, of rescuing a princess from a dragon, or, better, an unpredictable dream in which I do not know what will happen. Once this has started, I might get still more daring. I would wish to dream whole lifetimes, packing seventy years into a single night. I would dream that I am not dreaming at all, that I will never wake up, that I have completely lost myself somewhere down the tangled corridors of the mind, and, finally, that I am in such excruciating agony that when I wake up, it will be better than all possible dreams."

Alan Watts, *Eden*

THE FALL INTO A DIVIDED HERENOW

*In many cultures
the fall from paradise is also the loss
of godlike immortality.*

"AT FIRST no one needed to die," says a story told by the Gudji and Darasa tribes in Africa. "Then one day God wanted to see whether man or snake was worthy of immortality, and so he arranged a race between them. During the race the man met a woman. He stopped to smoke and chat with her for so long that the snake reached God first. And so God told man, 'The snake is worthier than you and it shall be immortal, but you shall die, and all your race.'"[4]

It is a matter of curiosity how much this story might have shifted toward blaming a woman for man's downfall as a consequence of contact with several generations of Christian missionaries to Africa. But the theme of a "fall" from paradise goes hand in hand with the Paradise myth itself, and is as universal. The cause of the fall in this African story is the attraction of the simple pleasures of the flesh, a smoke and an idle chat with a pretty woman. More common African myths are those which tell of a time when God was driven from the world by man's destructiveness in killing the animals, along with his general predisposition to assault and upset the balance of nature.

36

Adam and Eve represent "the fall," or the loss of
connection with the divine which is a theme
common to the mythologies around the world.

The marked difference between the two types of stories probably derives from the differences between nomadic and agricultural peoples. In fact, the immortal and worthy character of
the snake of the first type calls to mind some features of the ancient Mesopotamian myth of
Gilgamesh, as does the encounter with the woman. In the Gilgamesh tale she is both temptress
and wise woman, and advises Gilgamesh to abandon his quest for immortality. His single-point-
ed devotion to the quest is tested not in a race, but by an assignment to remain awake for six
days and seven nights. When he fails, the immortal Utanapishtim takes pity on him and offers
him a plant that restores youth – but this plant is stolen from the unfortunate Gilgamesh by a
serpent, as he bathes in a well.

Another common theme in mythologies of the fall of man is that of "forgetting" our true, immortal nature. In classical Greece this forgetfulness was represented by the River of Lethe.

In his book, *Memories and Visions of Paradise*, Richard Heinberg offers the compelling argument that, lying at the heart of virtually all myths of a fall from paradise, including the story of Adam and Eve in Genesis, can be found the idea that it was an attachment to one side of the coin – to the "fruits" of the phenomenal, physical world – which caused humankind to be separated from the divine and to lose the sacred sight of the whole. Or, in the words of Gautam Buddha, the truth that "in essence things are not two but one" has been subverted by the "false imagination" that we live in a dualistic world, and that we must cling to the part of it we know and inhabit. In our clinging, we both create and maintain the separation of heaven and earth, and prolong our exile from paradise.

Another persistent theme in the mythologies of the Fall is the theme of "forgetting." Like the Hindu conception of progressive decline through several "ages," from the Krita Yuga of perfection to the Kali Yuga of today, the Hopi Indians of North America also describe a progressive degeneration from an original, paradisal state. In the Hopi view, however, the entire world has been destroyed three times, each one marking an irreparable decline. In the original paradise world, everybody used to "remember" the plan of the Creator, the remembrance being facilitated by "keeping the door at the top of their heads open." At first a few, and then many people began to forget, and this first world had to be destroyed. At that time, those who "remembered" were escorted to a safe place so they could return and populate the next world. At the launching of the new world, they are told again to remember the Creator's plan, and to keep the "door at the top of their heads open" so that this remembrance can happen easily and without the distortions and temptations of everyday human life.[5]

This same theme of forgetting one's original identity and purpose is also found in the Hindu and Buddhist traditions, where the individual has, in a sense, fallen asleep and is lost in the dream of the physical world. In this sense, he or she is suffering from a separateness that exists only in the mind – and upon "waking" and discovering this separateness to be just a dream, the reality of oneness is regained in the here and now. With the awakened, immortal soul now directing our affairs, we can act out the play of the dream world in perfect harmony with the larger goals of existence itself.

The Gnostics of the first centuries of Christianity had a similar idea, and one of their central myths tells of a prince from the East who travels to Egypt to seek "the one pearl, which is in the midst of the sea around the loud-breathing serpent."[6] He is captured by the Egyptians and given a meal which makes him forget who he is, until at last his parents send him a letter which puts an end to his amnesia and enables him to capture the pearl and return home. Another variation on the "forgetting" motif is found in the Greek notion of the river of Lethe – the souls who drink from this "River of Forgetfulness" are in effect choosing mortality over immortality. They will be born having lost the memory not only of their own timeless identity but of the eternal truths known to mankind since the beginning. Thus all their learning in this life will be just a "recollection" of what they had known before, but have forgotten.

In *Phaedrus*, Plato both refers us to the Hermetic tradition and warns against the usefulness of mere scripture in our task of remembrance, when he sets up a dialogue between Thoth and Ammon. Thoth has been bragging about having invented the alphabet when Ammon rebukes him: "This discovery of yours will create forgetfulness in the learners' souls, because they will not use their memories; they will trust to the external, written characters and not remember of themselves. The specific which you have discovered is an aid not to memory but to reminiscence, and you give your disciples not truth, but only the semblance of truth; they will be hearers of many things and will have learned nothing; they will appear to be omniscient and will generally know nothing; they will be tiresome company, having the show of wisdom without its reality."[7]

In other words, once the ancient wisdom is divorced from the lifeblood of first-hand experience it becomes so much useless baggage. The ability to quote scripture and verse can be acquired through reading; the existential understanding of the ineffable truths the scriptures attempt to describe must be tasted in life. If our truths are to remain vital and relevant to the everchanging reality in which we live, they must be told again and again, within each successive generation, by those who *know* these truths and not by those who merely know *about* them. If this does not happen, if we must rely instead on the printed stories of those who lived centuries before us, we are denied the opportunity to "remember" the truth for ourselves, and to nourish its roots in the soil and climate of our own times.

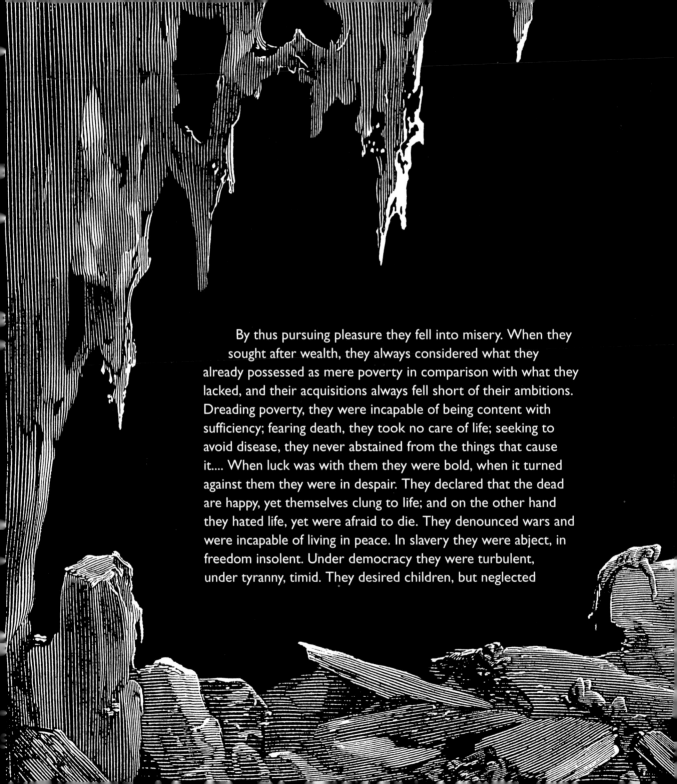

By thus pursuing pleasure they fell into misery. When they sought after wealth, they always considered what they already possessed as mere poverty in comparison with what they lacked, and their acquisitions always fell short of their ambitions. Dreading poverty, they were incapable of being content with sufficiency; fearing death, they took no care of life; seeking to avoid disease, they never abstained from the things that cause it.... When luck was with them they were bold, when it turned against them they were in despair. They declared that the dead are happy, yet themselves clung to life; and on the other hand they hated life, yet were afraid to die. They denounced wars and were incapable of living in peace. In slavery they were abject, in freedom insolent. Under democracy they were turbulent, under tyranny, timid. They desired children, but neglected

them when they had them. They
prayed to the gods, as to beings
able to assist them, and they
scorned them, as unable to punish;
or again, they feared them as
avenging powers, and swore
falsely, as if the gods had no
existence.

Maximus Tyrius, quoted in
Primitivism and Related Ideas in Antiquity
by Arthur Lovejoy and George Boas

> *Men fear death,*
> *as children fear to go in the*
> *dark; and as that natural fear in*
> *children is increased with tales,*
> *so is the other.*
>
> Francis Bacon, "Of Death,"
> *Essays* (1625)

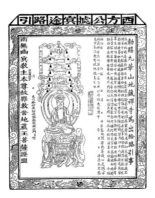

> *There is a dreadful Hell*
> *And everlasting pains;*
> *There sinners must*
> *with devils dwell*
> *In darkness, fire, and chains.*
>
> Isaac Watts, "Divine Songs for
> Children" (1720)

THE GEOGRAPHY OF THE HEREAFTER

*A Chinese "passport" to the next world, to be
burned as part of funeral ceremonies.
Opposite: Fears of divine punishment are reflected
in the near-universal mythology of a great flood.*

RICHARD HEINBERG also puts forward the idea that our collective memories of a "great flood" or similar natural catastrophe might have some basis in actual history, and that very real terrors are thereby lodged in the unconscious of us all. In any case, these "deluge myths" confirm the truth that until relatively recently in human history we have feared retribution and punishment for our misbehavior more in *this* life than we have feared that it will occur in the hereafter.

The ancients of Greece and Rome by and large tended to agree with the Old Testament notion that "dust thou art and to dust thou shalt return," at least as far as ordinary folk were concerned. And such heavens and hells as existed in the earliest scriptures of Eastern religions were either perceived as states of mind, or, at the most, temporary resting places in a very long journey towards reunion with the Absolute. For tribal peoples untouched by Christianity, the "hereafter" generally remained pretty much "here." Those who died rejoined the spirits, or the Great Spirit, whence they had come. And given the fact that those spirits were an integral part of the natural order of things here on earth there was, strictly speaking, no place to go. As Chief Seattle said, "There is no death, just a change of

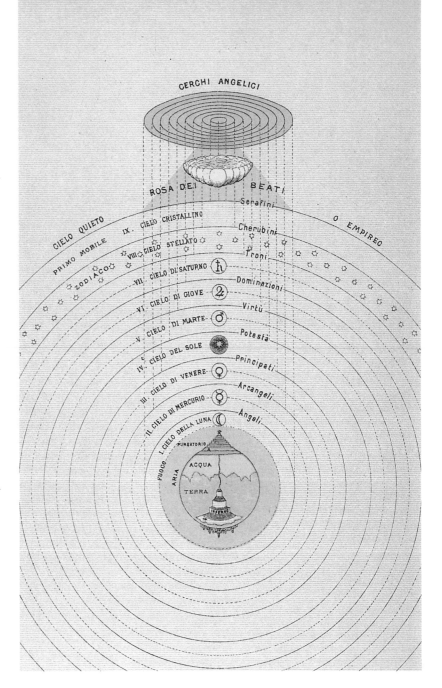

Reflecting the views of the theologians of his time, Dante portrayed both heaven and hell as multi-storied universes where people were sent to different levels according to the seriousness of their sins or the greatness of their virtue. Those who were forced to break religious vows, or who led exemplary lives but were nonetheless tainted by the desire for recognition, ...

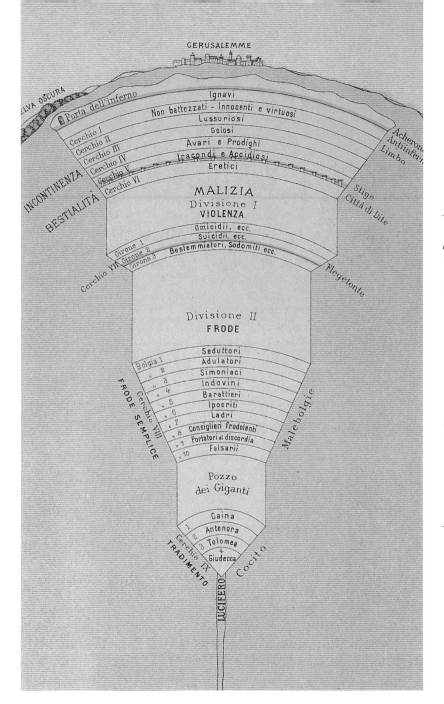

… for example, appeared to Dante in the "lower" realms of Paradise. Paradise was in reality not so stratified as Hell, however — there, the different types of sinners were very precisely defined, with traitors like Satan and Judas in the very depths of Hell, while those like Cleopatra, who were simply victims of their own human passions, were consigned to the shallower regions.

It seems to be a universal tendency of the human mind to try to make known what is unknowable. Ideas about the specific landscape of the hereafter have evolved over time.

worlds," and all worlds are present all the time for those who are sensitive enough to see them. The important thing was to mark the body's departure with proper ceremony and, in the cultures where bodies were buried, to make sure that they were not disturbed.

It wasn't until the first few centuries of Christianity that the awesome and physical landscapes of heaven and hell we are familiar with today began to be painted. In fact, most of the Bible is rather subdued when speaking of the afterlife, whether that life be "above" or "below." Revelation, the one apocryphal text which survived whatever squeamishness determined the final shape of the official Christian canon, only allows that bad people will be tormented in a "lake of fire and brimstone" in the end.

Apparently, this was not strong enough stuff to satisfy the later Christians' desire to know exactly what might await them if they strayed from the path. Relieved for the most part from the immediate threat of being ripped apart by wild animals for the amusement of the Romans, they began to specify the precise amount of wages to be extracted of unbelievers and potential miscreants. These elaborations on the biblical descriptions of the afterlife reached a peak in the Middle Ages and fueled an extraordinary interest both in the process of dying and what might await the departed in the world to come.

The earliest of these new extra-scriptural texts surfaced in Greece around the end of the third century. It claimed to be the record of an event referred to cryptically by St. Paul in

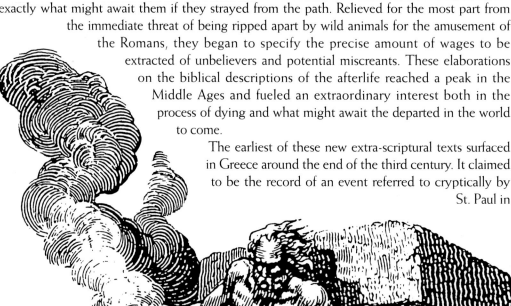

II Corinthians 12:2-3, where he says "I
know a man in Christ who fourteen years ago
was caught up into the third heaven – whether in the
body or out of the body I do not know, God knows. And I
know that this man was caught up into Paradise...and he heard things that cannot be told,
which man may not utter." This passage was commonly believed to be a reference to Paul's own
experience, not the experience of some other, anonymous "man in Christ." But 'The Vision of
St. Paul" circulated in third-century Greece cast aside whatever doubts might have remained,
along with Paul's reluctance to speak further about it. There are reasons to suspect that in fact
the tale was a Christian adaptation of Virgil's Aeneid. But its authenticity as an original historic
document was supported by claims that it had been found sealed in a marble box along with a
pair of Paul's shoes, and the text expanded his passing reference into a full-blown and detailed
account of a bodily visit not only to the heights of heaven but also to the depths of hell.

On his journey, Paul manages to introduce a Sabbath so that the unfortunate souls in hell
can enjoy an occasional day off from their otherwise eternal torment. It was a day off which
they certainly needed by the Middle Ages, when further elaborators on 'The Vision of St. Paul"
had done their work. Apparently following the journalistic maxim that good news is no news,
all references to heaven were excised. The torments of hell, on the other hand, had grown to
truly grotesque proportions. The flesh of ordinary sinners was nibbled by monstrous creatures,
they were suspended by their ears from flaming trees, pinned to the ground with red-hot nails,
and barbecued on flaming wheels. And those who were utterly beyond redemption were confined to a foul-smelling pit "sealed with seven seals."

Fortunately, this nasty place was a too extreme even for the most fire-breathing fundamen-
talist to inflict on everybody who was...well, just a little bit less than perfect. Maybe they only
broke a couple of commandments, and relatively small ones at that, like stealing a candy bar
from the corner shop when they were seven years old, or secretly coveting their neighbor's wife
when they were forty. Those types of smalltime sinners, who believed in God and Jesus all right
but just weren't sorry enough for their sins to confess them, or didn't have a chance to before
they died, eventually got a chance to make amends in Purgatory.

*The idea of Limbo was developed in response to the
need to deal fairly with virtuous unbelievers,
infants, and others who had no opportunity to
embrace the Christian faith before their deaths.*

This idea was first introduced by Pope Gregory in the sixth century, in his series of *Dialogues*. These works became immensely popular later in the Middle Ages, particularly the sections on "last things" which related deathbed visions and the experiences of those who had returned from the dead. It was here that Purgatory was first described in detail, according to firsthand information gathered by various people who had died and were revived. One account by a soldier tells us that this place was one where those in transition were challenged with the test of crossing a bridge: only if they were worthy would they make it to the paradise on the other side; otherwise they would fall into a horrible river full of demons. The soldier in Gregory's account witnessed an appropriate variety of these crossings to demonstrate to the readers both the wages of sin and the rewards of good behavior. And for good measure, he saw one unfortunate fellow who was the object of a tug-of-war between the demons of the stinking and infernal river of hell and the splendid, angel-like beings dressed in white who represented heaven. The soldier was called back to his body at the moment of greatest suspense, before learning the outcome. It was a twist to the plot which neatly served Gregory's instructive purposes in suggesting that there is still time for each of us to make sure that when our own time comes, the good guys win the battle. In inviting us to ponder the symbolic meaning of the story, Gregory points out that the angels were pulling on the man's hands, symbolizing the good of giving alms to the church, while the demons pulled on his legs which, it seems, must have carried him too often in pursuit of carnal pleasures.

Finally, even the unpleasantness of Purgatory, and the uncertain outcome of its trials, proved too severe for some cases. One couldn't in good conscience send an infant soul there, whose only sin was the "original" one that he or she hadn't even asked for. So the parents of these infants, along with many a Christian missionary confronted with the simple decency of those who nevertheless refused to be converted, have been comforted by the notion that such basically innocent souls will end up not in hell but in "limbo." Limbo is a rather nice park where they can enjoy themselves despite the fact that they are not allowed to mix with the elect in heaven. There, they will wait until Jesus himself can come back and clarify exactly what he meant by "whosoever believeth in me..." and sort out the rather sticky question of what to do with virtuous unbelievers, and those too young to believe anything at all.

54

PLAN
of the Road from
THE
City of Destruction
TO THE
CELESTIAL CITY.
Engraved expressly for
VIRTUE'S,
Elegant Edition of
THE
PILGRIMS PROGRESS.

Mistrust &
Timorous
meet Christian

Palace
called
Beautiful

VALLEY
OF HUMILIATION

Christian fights
with Appolyon

The Spies
meet Christian

---

*The geography of the hereafter, and its
correspondences to life on earth, has been a source
of endless fascination for artists and writers
throughout the ages.*

On the whole, Christianity has tended to be better at depicting hell than heaven or any of the other places. The demons and the tortures of hell have an immediacy and richness of texture generally lacking in the corresponding descriptions of heaven, which is most often some vague and ethereal place where angels sit around on clouds playing harps and singing hosannas. In the words of Francois Rene de Chateaubriand, "Heaven, where boundless felicity reigns, is too far above the human condition for the soul to be so strongly affected by the bliss of the elect: one can interest oneself but little in beings who are perfectly happy. This is why poets have succeeded better in the description of hells: at least humanity is there, and the torments of the guilty remind us of the miseries of our life."[8]

The Buddhists, on the other hand, go into elaborate and entrancing detail when describing their heaven. There are not simply rivers, but unbelievably clear rivers, with golden sand visible on the bottom. When one steps into them, their depth changes in response to one's wishes, from a refreshing footbath to a full-body soak. The temperature, too, is adjustable according to one's desire. "All the wishes those [heavenly] beings may think of, they will all be fulfilled, as long as they are rightful."[9] Never mind that Buddha himself preached an ultimate goal of nirvana, extinction of the individual personality and absolute freedom from any kind of desire at all, "rightful" or otherwise. His followers, although they may have loved the man, obviously found his vision a little unpalatable. After he had gone to his nirvana they promptly invented something more to their liking. If he hadn't been cremated but buried instead, Buddha would probably be turning in his grave.

Believe in something for another World
but don't be too set on what it is,
and then you won't start out that life
with a disappointment.

Will Rogers, *Autobiography*

WHO'S WHO
IN THE AFTERLIFE

A Native American burial ground where
the bodies of the dead are exposed to the
elements, while eagle feathers help to guide
the spirit on its way.

F IT IS DIFFICULT for a traveler to hidden realms to comprehend what he or she sees directly, it appears to be even
more difficult to tell others about it. Like all essentially spiritual experiences, we find ourselves forced to speak about
these journeys in metaphors – metaphors which have
appealed to the creative imaginations of writers and artists
throughout the ages. Our notions about the hereafter are
thus shaped by the imaginative flights of artistic genius –
from the ineffable, mysterious and unsayable experience
itself, they have woven colorful landscapes peopled by recognizable, if fantastic and otherworldly, forms. On these pages
is a sampling of just a few of the guides and guardians, angels
and demons, who have taken up residence in the hereafters
of different cultures over the ages.

WINGED ESCORTS
OF THE SOUL

The English word "angel" is derived from a Greek word meaning "messenger" and indeed, that is the role played by most of these winged beings in the Old and New Testaments of the Bible. Later, however, Judeo-Christian theology expanded the role of angels to include the special care of human souls, both as guardians on earth and as escorts to the celestial realms after death.

In Islam, there are two angels assigned to each individual during his or her lifetime – one to record good deads accomplished and the other to record sins. At death, the soul can expect to meet another pair of angels who will determine the soul's worthiness to enter paradise. This second pair of angels are rather fierce, and might even use the whips they carry in order to force the would-be entrant to paradise to tell the truth.

Some scholars speculate that the idea of angels has its roots in earlier times, when the task of conveying spirits to the other world was generally performed by birds. Many of the pre-European cultures of North and South America, for example, consider the eagle to be sacred – either as a messenger who conveys prayers to the spirit world and bestows blessings from it, or as a conveyor of the souls of the dead to the other world. The ancient Aztecs believed that the departed souls of warriors were transformed into eagles, who would then guard the sun. And both the Syrians and the early Romans believed that the eagle had a special responsibility for leading the souls of the worthy to paradise. The *ba*, one of many aspects of the soul according to the Egyptian view, was represented by a bird with a human head. The peacock, with its capacity to renew its magnificent plumage each year, became a Christian symbol for the resurrection.

The landscape and characters seen by Odysseus in
Hades reflected early beliefs about the afterlife.
Opposite: Charon's task is to ferry the souls of the
dead into the other world.

THE REALM OF THE SHADES

"Hades" was originally not only the "bad place" that it has come to be thought of today, but rather a gloomy place where the "shades" of all departed spirits, ended up, regardless of their deeds on earth. Their escort to this place was the boatman Charon, who ferried them across the river Styx in return for a fee, the coin for which was placed in the mouth of a corpse before it was buried.

From the realm of Hades, according to later classical mythologies, the spirits of the dead could be sent either to Elysium, the realm of the blessed, or to the infernal regions of Tartarus. This hereafter of classical mythology was named after the god who ruled it, who later came to

be known as Pluto. For six months of the year he was joined by his wife Persephone, whom he had abducted from the world above. Persephone's mother Demeter was so grieved by her daughter's abduction that she caused the earth to become barren so that no crops would grow. Finally a compromise was worked out, and Persephone was allowed to return to her mother for six months of the year, creating the seasons that we know now. Hades/Pluto was also understood to be the "giver of wealth" in the sense that crops grew from, and minerals were found in, the subterranean world which he governed. Only rarely would Hades allow anyone to escape from his realm, as he did when the hero/musician Orpheus played his lyre and caused Hades to "shed iron tears" in response to the beauty of the music. As a result, Orpheus was allowed to retrieve his dead wife Eurydice, but lost her again when his trust failed him. The test assigned to Orpheus by Hades was that he not look back as Eurydice followed him back to the world of the living, but Orpheus couldn't help himself and turned around at the last minute.

GUARDIANS OF THE GATE

The voracious three-headed Cerberus is perhaps the most famous "watchdog" guarding the gates to the other world, but he has counterparts in many other cultures. The abode of Yama, the Hindu god of death, is guarded by two fierce dogs with four eyes, who will eat the spirits of those who fail to run quickly enough to their destiny, and in ancient Egypt the souls who fail the test of the "weighing of the heart" are devoured by the monster Am-mut, a beast who is part crocodile, part lioness, and part hippopotamus.

AFTERLIFE ACCORDING TO DANTE

One of the most elaborate descriptions of the Christian hereafter has been given by the thirteenth-century Florentine poet Dante Alighieri, in his Divine Comedy. Embroidering his text with classical references and commentaries on famous political and religious figures of the day, Dante takes us through the many-layered landscapes of hell, purgatory and paradise under the guidance of the poet Virgil.

A fascinating story is told by Boccaccio about events surrounding Dante's own death, and the problem of the final cantos of his *Comedy* that his survivors were certain he had finished writing, but could find at the time. Apparently, Dante used to send sections of the completed work to his friend and patron Can Grande della Scala before making copies and distributing them to others. Before his death, all but the last thirteen cantos had been published in this way, and despite their certainty that Dante had finished them his sons Jacopo and Pietro could not find them anywhere. Encouraged by friends, Jacopo was just on the verge of attempting to finish the great work himself when, according to the legend, a vision of his father appeared to him in a dream. Boccaccio's account of the events is as follows:

"A worthy man of Ravenna, called Piero Giardino, who had been for a long time a pupil of Dante's, a sober-minded and trustworthy man, related that when eight months had elapsed from the day of his master's death, Jacopo di Dante came to his house one night, close upon the hour we call matins, and said that, that very night and a little before that hour, he had in his sleep seen his father Dante come to him, dressed in shining white garments and his face resplendent with unwonted light. And it seemed to him that he asked him whether he was alive, and heard him answer: 'Yes, but with the true life and not this of ours.' Wherefore he dreamed that he went on to ask whether he had finished his work before passing into the true life, and, if he had, where was the missing portion which they had never been able to find. To this he seemed, as before, to hear the answer: 'Yes, I finished it.' And then it seemed to him that he took him by the hand and led him into the room where he used to sleep when he lived in this life, and, touching one of the walls with his hand, said: 'Here is what you have been searching for so long.' And as soon as those words were spoken, it seemed to him that his sleep and Dante departed from him together. And so, he said, he could not wait, but had to come and tell him what he had seen, so that they might go together to look in the place shown to him (which remained very clearly impressed upon his memory) so as to see whether that which had so pointed it out was a true spirit or a false delusion...."

Boccaccio's account goes on to say that Jacopo and Giardino promptly went to the place where Dante had lived before his death, roused the current occupant, and found a cubbyhole in the wall behind a mat in the place Dante had pointed to in Jacopo's vision. "And in it they found a quantity of written sheets," says Boccaccio, "all mouldy with the dampness of the wall and ready to rot away if they had been left there any longer. When they had cleaned off all the mould, they saw that the pages were numbered and, having placed them in order, they found they had recovered, all together, the thirteen cantos that were lacking of the Comedy.... And thus the work which had taken so many years in the making was completed." [10]

Opposite: Peaceful and wrathful demons of the Tibetan Buddhists.
Left: A Chinese tomb guardian.
Right: Pottery figure of Mictlantecuhtli, Lord of the Dead in the Aztec culture, where the dead were reduced to skeletons by a wind of knives on their way to the other world.

Yea, though I walk through the valley of the shadow of death,
I will fear no evil: for thou art with me;
thy rod and thy staff they comfort me...

Psalm 23:4,
The Holy Bible

PEACEFUL AND WRATHFUL DEITIES

The imagery associated with death often seems designed to bring our fears to the surface so that we can learn to face them, and earlier cultures made use of this fearful imagery far more often than we do today. For the Tibetans, the challenge at death is to encounter all such images with the same equanimity, realizing that all external forms are just projections of the mind.

Many cultures also use frightening images to adorn the resting places of the dead. These statues, masks, and effigies serve as a warning to the living against desecrating or otherwise disturbing the gravesites, lest they also meet with the same fate as its current occupants. They may also be used to appease and flatter the god or gods whose responsibility it is to look after the spirits of the dead, so that they will enjoy a good "life" in the world beyond.

KNOCKING ON HEAVEN'S DOOR

On their journeys into death, the Egyptians at the time of the Middle Kingdom (about 2040-1786 BC) expected to meet first with Osiris and forty-two gods who served as a tribunal and would judge their deeds in life. The heart of the dead person was put on a set of scales to be weighed against the single ostrich feather worn by Maat, daughter of the sun god Re and goddess of truth. If the heart was heavier than the feather, it would be devoured by the hybrid monster Am-mut.

Egyptologists have speculated that one of the practices of the cult of Osiris was to intentionally provoke a near-death experience as part of the initiation of a new king. The man would taken to the depths of the Great Pyramid, where he was placed inside a sarcophagus which was then sealed with wax. The sarcophagus remained sealed precisely long enough for the initiate to "die" before the seal was broken and the lid thrown open so that the sudden rush of oxygen could revive him. These initiates would apparently often report traveling through a tunnel towards a bright light where they received confirmation of immortality from a radiant being dressed in white. "No man escapes death," says one passage from the texts related to this mystery rite, "and every living soul is destined to resurrection. You go into the tomb alive that you will learn of the light."[11] In partaking of this ritual, each new king—who was believed to be the physical reincarnation of the god Osiris—was re-enacting the original death of Osiris at the hands of Seth, who sealed him inside a sarcophagus and threw it into the Nile.

2

LIFE AFTER LIFE
AFTER LIFE AFTER LIFE

The mere fact that people talk about rebirth, and that there is such a concept at all, means that a store of psychic experiences designated by that term must actually exist.
Rebirth is an affirmation that must be counted among the primordial affirmations of mankind.

Carl Gustav Jung

OPPORTUNITIES MISSED AND SECOND CHANCES

THE HEREAFTER visions of Christianity, Judaism and Islam are profoundly shaped by the idea common to these three religions that there is only one life in the body. Of the three, only Christianity has expended such a great deal of effort to define what awaits the soul after death. Both Islam and Judaism have developed ideas of an immortal soul, and punishment or reward for the actions or beliefs of this soul after death, but the primary interest of both religions is focused on creating the lost paradise here on earth.

The belief in just one life, combined with a belief in the immortality of the soul, creates as a logical consequence the belief in an everlasting punishment or reward for that soul's actions in its lifetime. We get just one opportunity to claim our place among the saved or the damned, and if we blow it, we have blown it forever. It seems a little unfair, and Christianity in particular

*Eastern religious traditions say that we pass
through many bodies on a path of spiritual
development until we are finally rid of all the desires
that might bring us back into the material realm.*

has tried to devise ways to ameliorate the unfairness by giving the departed souls a chance to work their way from one side of the dividing line to the other in purgatory. Muslims are also given a posthumous opportunity to declare their faith in Allah, and the Jews have the comfort of knowing that they are special favorites of God in the first place, and so have very little to worry about.

The Eastern religions of Hinduism and Buddhism, on the other hand, see life on earth as a kind of "school for souls." We are sent back again and again, as many times as needed to learn our lessons and move on. There is a popular misconception that Buddha himself did not believe in reincarnation, a misconception that probably arises from the fact that his teachings emphasized the extinction of individual personality, its ego and desires. Like Jesus, Mohammed, Moses, and other great spiritual teachers, Buddha spoke in the context of his times. He was born into a world defined by the framework of Hinduism, and into a culture where the popular tendency was to rigidify the teachings of the ancients into formulas and superstitions that had very little if anything to do with the state of choiceless awareness that he was trying to promote. As an antidote to these popular tendencies, more greedy than spiritual, to pile up good deeds in the karmic account to gain a better life the next time around, he insisted on getting out of the game altogether. Mostly, when Buddha was asked questions about the afterlife, he simply refused to answer.

That leads to another source of many misconceptions about both Hinduism and Buddhism, which is the fact that in the East it has always been the custom to embroider, debate, and comment upon existing spiritual teachings. There is not one Bible, one Koran, one Torah in the East – there is, rather, a rich and often contradictory library of literally thousands of texts, many of which have formed the basis for various sects and subdivisions of adherence to the original teachings on which they were based. Buddhism, for example, differs radically in both practice and doctrine from Sri Lanka to Tibet, from Thailand to China, from Burma to Japan. Hinduism contains the teachings of Manu alongside the heroic legends of the Mahabharata, and embraces the sermons of the Bhagavad Gita together with the lyric poetry of the Upanishads. In the East, the emphasis is on the spiritual journey itself, and the only certainty is that eventually, even if it takes an unimaginable length of time, all paths will lead all souls to the same, transcendent goal.

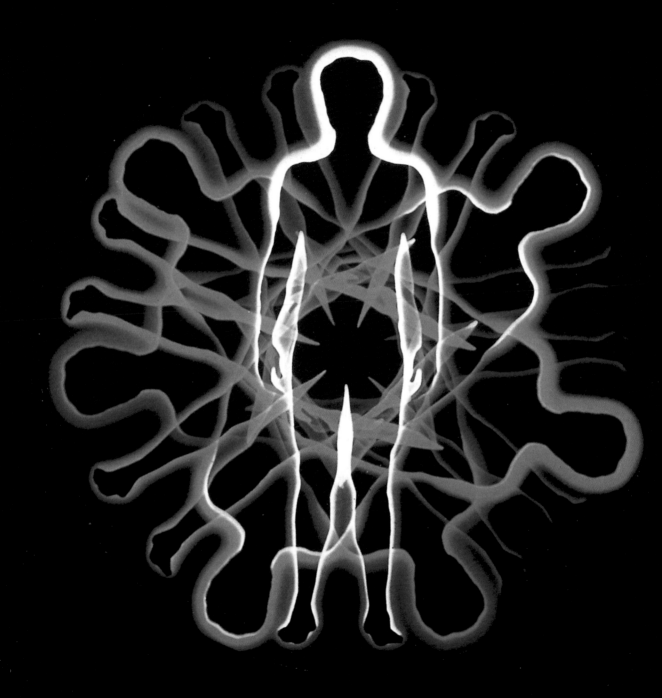

A story is told about Gautam Buddha that clearly illustrates the difference between his approach to questions of death and immortality and the approach of Jesus as reported in the Christian gospels. The story from Buddha's life follows.

THAT WHICH NEVER DIES

A woman goes to Buddha: her child is dead and she is crying and weeping. She is a widow and she will never have another child, and the only child is dead, and was the object of all her love and all her attention, and she wanted Buddha to bring the child back to life. But what did Buddha do? Buddha smiled and said to her, "You go into the town and just find a few mustard seeds from a house where nobody has ever died."

And the woman rushed into the town, and she went to each house. And wherever she went they said, 'We can give you as many mustard seeds as you want, but the condition will not be fulfilled – because so many people have died in our house." Again and again it happened.

But she hoped, "Maybe...who knows? There may be some house somewhere that has not known death." And she went around and around the whole day. By the evening a great understanding had dawned on her: Death is a part of life. It happens. It is not something personal, it is not a personal calamity that has happened to me. With that understanding she went back to Buddha.

He asked, "Where are the mustard seeds?"

And she smiled and she fell at his feet and she said, "Initiate me. I would like to know that which never dies. I don't ask for my child back, because even if he is given to me, he will die again. Teach me something so that I can know inside myself that which never dies."

From *The Wisdom of the Sands*, Volume I by Osho

The soul is the Perceiver;
is assuredly vision itself
pure and simple,
unmodified;
and looks directly
upon ideas.
For the sake of the soul
alone, the Universe exists.

The Yoga Sutras of
Patanjali

The Lord is hidden
in every heart.
He is the eternal witness...
Watching our work
from within
As pure consciousness.

Shvetashvatara
Upanishad

YOGA: THE SCIENCE OF THE SOUL

THE MOST difficult thing for most Westerners to grasp in the wisdom traditions of the East is the idea of "soul" as Patanjali, among others, describes it. If the soul (or, as it is more commonly translated, the Self with a capital S) travels through many lives, for the purpose of eventual reunion with its divine source, then it becomes important to identify this entity and do our best to put it in charge of our affairs. Another way of putting it is to say that one must learn to shift one's identity and sense of "self" away from the transient body and its thoughts and preoccupations and towards the eternal, unchanging "Perceiver" of the world through which this body-mind complex is passing. Once the shift is complete, the lessons have been learned and there is no need to come back to school again.

Patanjali again: "By concentrating his mind upon the true nature of the soul as being entirely distinct from any experiences, and disconnected from all material things, and dissociated from the understanding, a knowledge of the true nature of the soul itself arises." To the average

*According to Patanjali and other sages of the East,
the soul, or "Self" travels through many lives
towards eventual reunion with its divine source.*

Western mind this is dense stuff, to say the least, if not outright gobbledygook. But that's just the sort of problem one runs into when trying to explain what it's like to be God. Quite frankly, it's pretty dense stuff for the average Eastern mind to comprehend as well – which is why Buddha, and those who developed his teachings in the direction of Zen, laid so much emphasis on doing away with the mind altogether. Any idea that we can have about the nature of the transcendent unity of reality automatically separates us from it, the way a comma separates a clause in a sentence.

Only by getting rid of *all* our ideas – in Patanjali's words, becoming "dissociated from the understanding" – can we perceive the truth of the situation. "Through a glass darkly, and then face to face," says the Bible, to use a more familiar language. This is the language of mystics in all traditions, not only those of the East. It is just that the Eastern traditions tend to place the mystic experience at the center of the religious stage, rather than confining it to the secret chambers of the initiated few.

If we accept that the soul must evolve and learn to finally unite itself with the divine, then it follows that there must be a lesson plan. Patanjali's work offers perhaps the most comprehensive and scientific lesson plan ever devised for such a journey. It takes into account the different evolutionary stages and predispositions of the individual souls, and offers a choice of paths through psychophysical exercises, work, knowledge, or devotion. And, as Huston Smith points out in his *World's Religions,* this privilege of choice is accorded only to those who have reached the human bodily form. "On the subhuman level the passage is through a series of increasingly complex bodies until at last a human one is attained," he explains. "Up to this point the soul's growth is virtually automatic. It is as if the soul were growing as steadily and normally as a plant and receiving at each successive embodiment a body which, being more complex, provides the needed largesse for its new attainments. With the soul's graduation into a human body this automatic, escalator mode of ascent comes to an end. Its assignment to this exalted habitation is evidence that the soul has reached self-consciousness, and with this estate come freedom, responsibility, and effort."

Contrary to popular belief, very few of the central doctrines of the East preach a "devolution" of the soul into animal or insect bodies as punishment for bad behavior. The use or abuse

of the human freedom to make choices about how to behave does indeed create "karma," but that karma must be either enjoyed or suffered in both this and in future human lives. Although the *Tibetan Book of the Dead* does mention the possibility of taking birth in the animal kingdom, this is meant as metaphor, a device to startle the dying human into alertness. Apart from such devices and metaphors, most interpreters of Eastern scriptures would say that it is a fundamental misunderstanding of the function of karma in relation to human freedom to think that a soul would be sent back to an unconscious, pre-human state. To return to the analogy of life as a school, the lessons may have to be repeated if they are not learned, but one is never expelled from school and forced to start all over again. The *Brihadaranyaka Upanishad* explains it thus:

"As a person acts, so he becomes in life. Those who do good become good; those who do harm become bad. Good deeds make one pure; bad deeds make one impure. So we are said to be what our desire is. As our desire is, so is our will. As our will is, so are our acts. As we act, so we become. We live in accordance with our deep, driving desire. It is this desire at the time of death that determines what our next life is to be. We will come back to earth to work out the satisfaction of that desire."

*The soul passeth
from form to form;
and the mansions of her
pilgrimage are manifold.
Thou puttest off thy
bodies as raiment;
and as vesture dost thou
fold them up.
Thou art from old,
O Soul of Man; yea,
thou art from everlasting.*
The Books of Hermes
Trismegistus

*"Every soul comes into this
world strengthened by
the victories or weakened by
the defeats of its previous life.
Its place in this world as
a vessel appointed to honor or
dishonor is determined by its
previous merits or demerits. Its
work in this world determines
its place in the world which is
to follow this..."*
Origen (185-254 AD),
De Principiis

AN IDEA THAT REFUSES TO DIE

*Origen was one of the early Church Fathers who
believed in reincarnation. Opposite: Socrates was
another who appeared to believe that our
development takes place over several lifetimes.*

THE VARIOUS moves toward consolidating the Church in the early centuries of Christianity did such an effective job of eradicating belief in reincarnation – a belief which many in the Church hierarchy considered to be pagan and against Catholic doctrine – that most of us now tend to think of it as an exclusively Eastern idea. In fact the idea is too elegant, and offers too many appealing explanations for the paradoxes and inequities to be found in human life, to have been confined only to one hemisphere of the planet. It is a recurring theme in what survives of the teachings of the Middle Eastern and Greek mystery schools; Pythagoras, for example, is said to have made frequent reference to his own past lives, and to have been able to describe the past lives of his disciples. Plato speaks frequently of his belief that we pass through many bodies in our journey towards ultimate fulfillment, and he echoes the familiar warning of his teacher Socrates against becoming more interested in the pursuits of the body than in the quest of the "true philosopher": "Each pleasure and pain, having a nail, as it were, nails the soul to the body," he says, "and causes it to become corporeal, deeming those things to be true what-

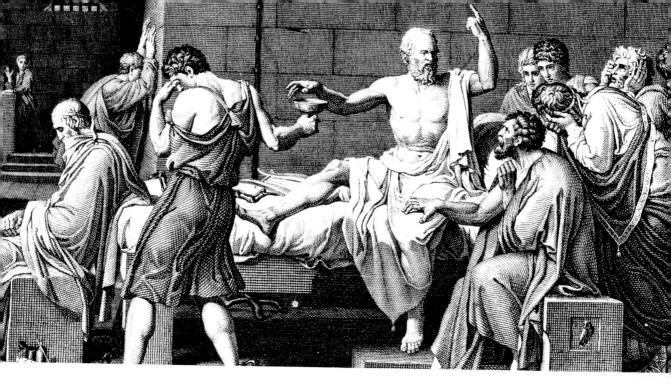

ever the body asserts to be so. [In such circumstances] it can never pass into Hades in a pure state, but must ever depart polluted by the body, and so quickly falls into another body."[1] In his *Laws*, he echoes the Eastern idea of karma when he says that "if you become worse you will go to the worse souls, or if better to the better, and in every succession of life and death you will do and suffer what like may fitly suffer at the hands of like."

Records of the early centuries of Christianity are full of references to doctrinal squabbles with the neo-Platonists, whose influence was powerful enough to give new meaning to the life of Augustine before he finally converted to Christianity and became a saint. In his *Confessions*, remnants of the attraction remain, as he laments that he has "neither father nor mother, nor experience of others, nor mine own memory" to answer his question, "Did my infancy succeed another age of mine that died before it?...Was I anywhere or in any body?" But the matter was settled for Christians, at least in terms of the official Catholic doctrine, when the Fifth Ecumenical Council was convened in 553 AD by the Emperor Justinian. During this council a number of "anathemas" were issued, clearly intended to deal with the pagans once and for all. Among the "anathematized" were the teachings of the much-venerated early Church Father Origen, along with all other teachings that suggested the pre-existence of the soul in any form. The position of the council was that the only view of immortality possible was that of bodily

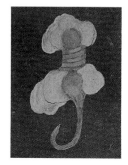

resurrection at Judgment Day, in human form, to go either to a permanent heaven or be confined to a permanent hell. Various sects of Christianity, including the Gnostics, the Cathars, the Waldensians and Priscillians, subsequently challenged this view, but with a resounding and sometimes fatal (corporeally speaking, at least) lack of success.

Elsewhere, and in other times, the Druids for example believed that there were three worlds – one of happiness above, one of misery below, and this one, where good and evil are absolutely balanced and human beings have absolute freedom to choose between the two. Depending on their choices, people were sent after death to one of the other two worlds as reward or punishment, to further purify the soul in preparation for its next incarnation. The Druids' belief in reincarnation was so strong in fact that they were even known to borrow money or goods in the present life with a promise of repayment in the next. The ultimate aim of all these lifetimes, and the visits to "heaven" and "hell" in between, was to attain unity with God – a unity that was ultimately everybody's destiny, though some might have to return many times before their souls were sufficiently purified.

Countless other examples can be found from ancient cultures all over the world, and one study published by the Theosophists asserts that no less than a hundred different, widely scattered tribal or primitive peoples can be identified who believe in reincarnation in some form. As Jung suggested, the idea seems to rest in the collective unconscious right alongside Paradise, the Fall, and our hoped-for return to innocence.

The idea that one might look favorably upon an ultimate escape from life embodied on earth might be alien to most Westerners, but it is a central theme in the teachings of cultures that believe in reincarnation. There are many obstacles to this ultimate union with the divine, including the greed for the event itself, as this story illustrates.

The great sage Narada was known as a traveler who was able to commune with the heavens, and one day as he was passing through a forest he saw a man who had been meditating for so long that ants had built a huge mound around his body. When the man saw Narada, he asked, "Where are you going?"

"I am going to heaven," replied Narada.

"In that case I have a favor to ask of you," said the man. "Please ask the God of Heaven when he will be merciful to me and allow me to attain freedom from rebirth."

Narada agreed, and continuing on his journey met a second man. "Narada," said the second man, "where are you going?"

"I am going to heaven," Narada answered.

"Will you do me the favor of asking," pleaded the second man, "when I shall attain freedom from rebirth?"

Narada agreed, and continued on his journey to heaven. Upon his return, he once again passed the man he had met first on the way. The mound built by the ants around the meditator's unmoving body had grown even higher. "Narada," the man called out. "Did you ask about me?"

"Yes," Narada responded. "And the God of Heaven said that you would attain freedom in four more births."

The man began to weep and wail, "I can't bear it! God is so cruel to me! I have meditated until an anthill has been raised around me, and I have yet four more births to endure!"

Narada passed down the road and met the second man.

"Did you ask about me?" he wanted to know.

"Yes, I did," replied Narada. "Do you see this tamarind tree? I'm afraid I must tell you that as many leaves as there are on that tree, so many times you will be born, and only then will you attain freedom."

The man began to dance for joy, shouting, "God is so merciful to me! After so short a time I shall be free!"

At that moment, a voice was heard coming from heaven, saying, "My child, you shall have freedom this very instant!"

Adapted from the *Kurma Purana*

Now, when all the souls had chosen their lives...
they all traveled into the plain of Lethe...
In the evening they encamped by the Forgetful River, whose water no pitcher can hold.
And all were compelled to drink a certain measure of its water;
and those who had no wisdom to save them drank more than the measure.
And as each man drank he forgot everything.
When they had gone to rest, and it was now midnight,
there was a clap of thunder and an earthquake;
and in a moment the souls were carried up to their birth, this way and that, like shooting stars.

Plato, *The Republic*, Book X

FIRSTHAND EXPLORATIONS OF THE DISTANT PAST

Most cultures view the journey from life to death as some kind of "crossing." Those who believe in reincarnation say that the memory of the previous life is reserved to the most advanced souls.

IF WE HAVE indeed passed through many lives, why don't we remember them? Because, the ancient wisdom says, we are made forget, to "drink the waters of Lethe" before we are born again, so that our remembrance won't spoil the whole game. Besides, one can imagine – it is difficult enough sometimes to comprehend events and their meanings in *this* life, never mind having to deal with a whole queue of lifetimes stretching back only God knows how far into the past.

Nevertheless, it seems that sometimes a returning soul escapes the net and comes into this world still carrying his or her memories. The nineteenth-century traveler Laurence Oliphant describes one such case he encountered in his visits with the Druses in Syria. The Druse, a sect founded in the eleventh century by a man claiming to be the reincarnated uncle of Mohammed, are thought by some scholars to be descended from a group of persecuted mystics who fled to the mountains of Syria during the early years of Christianity. Oliphant, in his book *The Land of Gilead, with Excursions in the Lebanon*, tells the story of a five-year-old boy who, finding himself

people in ordinary occupations. Most often, the memories were of some kind of crisis in the life of the former personality, and in many cases they touched on the moment of death. Some of the therapists who found themselves listening to these fascinating stories decided to look into the matter further, and eventually a whole new area of therapy was born.

Most past-life therapists are content to put the question of the "truth" of past life recall aside. They say that the effectiveness of the treatment in resolving the dilemmas of this life is sufficient reason in itself to use past life regression as therapy, and the issue of whether these memories are "real" or in some way "imaginary" is largely irrelevant. Others, more oriented toward research, have begun to collect these stories and to sort out the ones that cannot be explained away by any of the usual criteria of unconscious memory or imagination.

Among these researchers are Raymond Moody, whose earlier work had led to the publication of *Life After Life*, the book most often credited with sparking the current wave of interest in the near-death experience. After the publication of his book, he received hundreds of letters from people reporting their own experiences, and among these were dozens who told of vivid memories of their own past lives. His research into the phenomenon of past life recall started in earnest after a friend and colleague persuaded him to set aside his skepticism and undergo a past-life regression session himself. What he experienced in this and subsequent sessions was so extraordinary that he decided to apply the same methods he had used in his near-death research to construct a model of the past-life experience.

It is not an extraordinarily rigorous model, and perhaps cannot be, given the experience it attempts to describe. But along the way, Moody did discover a number of cases that defied all objections raised by the critics. One case typical of these is that of a Native American artist in the Southwest, who began speaking French during a past life regression. This put the hypnotherapist at an obvious disadvantage, so he asked his subject to translate. The man then began to speak in English but with a pronounced and seemingly authentic French accent. He was a composer in Paris, he said, and gave his name and a date in the eighteenth century. The story of his life was told in great detail, as he spent his days working on his music and his nights in the Paris cafes. He could, and did, go back and forth at will between English and French even though in "real life" he had never studied the French language.

The usual psychological explanation for this phenomena is "xenoglossia," which asserts that when people are able to speak a language they do not consciously know, it is because they have been exposed to this language at some time but have simply forgotten it. However, the hypnotherapist in this case was unable to find that his subject had had any previous exposure to the French language whatsoever. And further research into his story led to the discovery of references to the French composer and his work in a music library.

It is a telling fact that even past-life therapists themselves are reluctant to argue that the results they achieve in their sessions are "proof" that we have all lived many times before. Our culture carries a deep-seated fear and mistrust of hypnosis, even today, when it has finally been accepted as a valid means of treating any number of physical and psychological disorders. And, remembrance of "past lives" in recent decades has become inextricably bound up in a number of other "New Age" fashions which tend to make it guilty by association with all sorts of ideas we consider to be too "flaky" to take seriously. The innocent young children studied by Ian Stevenson are easier to believe, and his rigorous methods of research harder to discount. But for those who would like to explore the question for themselves, Moody offers a number of methods in his book, *Life Before Life*. And, as he did with his near-death research, he provides a "model" to check one's experiences against those of others, shown overleaf.

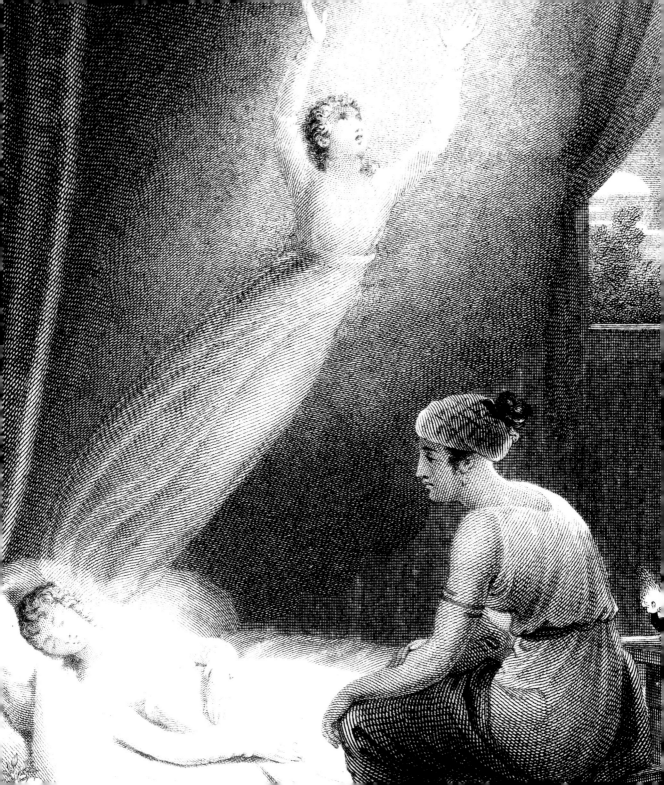

THE PAST LIFE EXPERIENCE

In recent years, many people have begun to use hypnosis to get through the barrier that normally separates us from memories of past lives. From his study of these experiences, Raymond Moody has developed the following list of traits common to these "past life regressions."

THE EXPERIENCE IS USUALLY VISUAL

... and is perceived by the subject to be more vivid and "real" than ordinary daydreams, and without the bizarre distortions of the dreams that occur in sleep.

PAST-LIFE REGRESSIONS SEEM TO HAVE A LIFE OF THEIR OWN

The person experiencing them does not feel that they are "making them up" as they go along, or directing their outcome in any way. On the contrary, the feeling is as if one is "watching a movie."

THE IMAGERY HAS AN UNCANNY FEELING OF FAMILIARITY

Subjects report that they feel as if they have already experienced what is taking place, as in the experience known as *déjà vu*.

THE SUBJECT IDENTIFIES WITH ONE CHARACTER

There is no question of changing roles within the unfolding scene, and it is clear to the subject who he or she is, despite the fact that the past life personality may be a different gender or have a dramatically different identity than the present one.

PAST LIFE EMOTIONS MAY BE (RE)EXPERIENCED DURING A REGRESSION

Subjects almost always report that they feel the emotions related to the experience they are witnessing, sometimes so strongly that the hypnotherapist must reassure and remind them that the event is in the past and there is no longer any need to be frightened, or angry, or sad.

PAST-LIFE EVENTS MAY BE VIEWED IN TWO DISTINCT PERSPECTIVES – FIRST- AND THIRD-PERSON

Subjects may even switch back and forth, from observing the scene as a spectator, to being "inside" the heads of their past-life personalities.

THE EXPERIENCE OFTEN MIRRORS PRESENT ISSUES IN THE SUBJECT'S LIFE

This is one of the main justifications for the use of past-life regression in therapy, and one of the most compelling reasons to argue that the scenes being witnessed by subjects are simply a kind of psychological theater, "made up" from elements of current, deeply felt dilemmas. At the same time, those who believe these experiences are "real" argue that it makes perfect sense that we should carry deep-seated problems from one life to the next, since our main purpose in living is to work free of all such problems.

REGRESSION MAY BE FOLLOWED BY GENUINE IMPROVEMENT IN MENTAL STATE

Whether the experiences are "real" or not, their effect on helping the subject to resolve his or her present conflicts, or to put them in perspective, is often dramatic.

REGRESSIONS MAY AFFECT MEDICAL CONDITIONS

Especially in cases of psychosomatic illnesses, reliving a past life experience related to the present condition can alleviate or dissolve the symptoms.

REGRESSIONS DEVELOP ACCORDING TO MEANINGS NOT HISTORICAL TIME

When subjects travel through several past lives, their sequence is not always chronological. And, the events witnessed are not random and unrelated, but tend to move through certain themes related to the progress of an individual's spiritual and psychological development.

PAST-LIFE REGRESSIONS BECOME EASIER WITH REPETITION

As with most unfamiliar journeys, this one tends to get easier with practice.

MOST PAST LIVES ARE MUNDANE

Most past-life regression therapists say that their patients usually find themselves to be ordinary people in their past lives – sometimes to their disappointment!

from *Life Before Life,* by Raymond Moody Jr., M.D.

The human being has two states of consciousness:
one in this world, the other in the next.
But there is a third state between them,
not unlike the world of dreams,
in which we are aware of both worlds,
with their sorrows and joys.
When a person dies, it is only the physical body that dies;
that person lives on in a nonphysical body,
which carries the impressions of his past life.
It is these impressions that determine his next life.
In this intermediate state he makes and dissolves impressions by the light of the Self.

Brihadaranyaka Upanishad

LIFE BETWEEN LIFE?

The growth in the practice of hypnotic regression
therapy has led some therapists to explore past lives
and even to try to discover what might happen
between the time of death and rebirth.

THE FACT that people appear to be able to regress to past lives has led other researchers to explore whether we might be able to retrieve some memory of what happens to us between lives as well. Joel Whitton, a Toronto psychiatrist who has done extensive research in using hypnosis to investigate the possibility of reincarnation, has had remarkable success in regressing his subjects to the "in between" state, and many of their descriptions match those of people who have been clinically dead and brought back to life. "It's so bright, so beautiful, so serene," they say. "It's like going into the sun and being absorbed without any sensation of heat. You go back to the wholeness of everything. I didn't want to come back."[3]

Of course, people in trance are able to spend as long as they like in this place, and their reports have enabled Whitton – and the rest of us – to speculate on what might happen after death, to those who are not sent back to live in their existing bodies but are allowed to stay on

and prepare for their next incarnation. According to Whitton, the time we spend between lives may be as little as ten months (earth time, presumably) or as long as eight hundred years. Those who are not particularly interested in their own spiritual development and growth spend much of this time in a kind of stupor until they are roused for their next incarnation. The rest, depending on their commitment to their own growth, spend their time in study and preparation for their next life. Whitton's subjects report that they are literally given the opportunity to determine their own fates: "I am being helped to work out the next life so that I can face whatever difficulties come my way," reports one person from his entranced state. "I don't want to take the responsibility because I feel that I don't have the strength. But I know we have to be given obstacles in order to overcome those obstacles – to become stronger, more aware, more evolved, more responsible."

It is also in this state that one's "karma" becomes clear, and plans are made to act in accordance with it. "There are people I didn't treat too well in my past life, and I have to go back to the Earth plane again and work off the debt. This time, if they hurt me in return, I'm going to forgive them because all I really want to do is go back home. This is home." According to Whitton, the more "advanced" souls might plan several lifetimes at once, mapping out a course of learning for themselves designed to lead them to a distant goal. Thus some of the lifetimes they plan may even include purposeful suffering in order to gain the necessary insight or compassion, for example, needed for the more distant goal.

3

SOUL SEARCHING

"SURVIVAL" – THE SECULAR VIEW

THE SEARCH for the soul, or more particularly what happens to it after we die, has taken many forms throughout human history. Apart from the strictly religious or spiritual search, there are countless references to ghosts, spirits, and other forms of "wandering souls" in both recorded and oral histories of virtually every tribe and culture on the planet. In our own culture, there was an outbreak of interest in the subject during the last century which spread so far and wide that Conan Doyle was moved to say that it was as if a "psychic cloud" had descended on the earth, creating very unusual weather indeed.

In 1848, a series of strange events took place in upstate New York, centering around a house that had long been reputed to be "haunted." Investigators were called in, and the developments which followed their investigations triggered a widespread interest in the question of what came to be rather bleakly called "survival." This interest, fueled by the eternal human fascination with ghosts, eventually grew into a movement known as Spiritualism, complete with its own study groups and churches. It is a movement which still survives today, especially in England – a notoriously "haunted" country – where Spiritualist congregations claim some 200,000 members.

The new inhabitants of the haunted house in New York, the Fox family, had barely settled in when they began to hear strange noises, including loud bangs, knocking, rapping, and what sounded like furniture being dragged across the floor. Two of the Fox's six living children, fifteen-year-old Margaret and twelve-year-old Kate, were more intrigued by the phenomena than frightened, and soon began to play games with this entertaining "poltergeist." Their mother described one incident in a sworn statement:

Daniel Dunglass Home's extraordinary seances
earned him worldwide notoriety.
Opposite: The Fox sisters, whose childhood games
launched a wave of interest in Spiritualism.

"On Friday night, March 31, 1848...it commenced as usual. I knew it from all the other noises I had ever heard before. The children, who slept in the other bed in the room, heard the rappings, and tried to make similar sounds by snapping their fingers. My youngest child said: 'Mr. Splitfoot, do as I do,' clapping her hands. The sounds instantly followed her with the same number of raps. When she stopped the sound ceased for a short time. Then Margaret said, in sport, 'Now, do just as I do: Count one, two three, four,' striking one hand against the other at the same time; the raps came as before.... I then thought I could put a test that no one in the place could answer. I asked the noise to rap my different children's ages, successively. Instantly each one of my children's ages was given correctly, pausing between them suffi-ciently long to individualize them until the seventh, at which a longer pause was made, and then three more emphatic raps were given, corresponding to the age of the little one that died... I then asked: 'Is this a human being that answers my questions...?' There was no rap... 'Is it a spir-it? If it is, make two raps.' The sounds were given as soon as the request was made."[1]

The family soon devised a code to use in communicating with the spirit – each letter of the alphabet was assigned a different number of raps, along with a code for yes and no. Through their communications they learned that the spirit belonged to a man who had been murdered in the house. He named his murderer, and told the family where his body was buried. Early efforts to uncover the spirit's bodily remains were hampered by the waterlogged condition of the soil under the house, and presumably the family's reluctance to cause structural damage in the process of the search. But eventually an excavation of the cellar uncovered human bones, fol-lowed by the discovery, in 1904, of the full skeleton.

Meanwhile, the Fox sisters were giving public demonstrations of their ability to make their spirit friend perform as they wished, and even taking him along with them on journeys to New

York City. Within just a few years the idea had caught on, and hundreds of "mediums" as they were called, were demonstrating similar abilities – although with the help of different spirits, of course – in private drawing rooms and public theaters all over Europe and North America. As for the Fox sisters, Kate eventually gave a public demonstration of how she had created rapping noises by manipulating the joints of her toes, one of many "exposures" that had all but put the Spiritualists out of business permanently by the end of the century.

Kate Fox later claimed that she had been bribed into making her "confession" and that although her demonstration had been real enough, the spirits were even more real and ought to be taken as such. Her assertion cannot be dismissed out of hand – many other mediums of the day admitted that, under pressure to perform and finding their spirits unavailable, they had learned to duplicate some of the effects which under more relaxed circumstances really did come from the "spirits." But the scales had already been tipped in favor of the opinion that all such communications with the "other side" were fraudulent and could be explained as no more than skillful conjuring tricks.

In the heyday of Spiritualism, though, mediums who claimed to be able to communicate with spirits, or even to call up apparitions of the dead, soon found that they were in constant demand, if nothing else as sources of entertainment. Some mediums were able to speak in languages they had never learned and others, connecting with dead composers, were adept at playing musical instruments on which they could hardly manage when not in a mediumistic trance. Of the many thousands of mediums who flourished during the latter half of the nineteenth century, some reached international fame. Daniel Dunglass Home, for example, emerged unblemished from numerous careful investigations by skeptics hoping to prove that the spectacular phenomena produced at his seances were fraudulent. Among other things, he was apparently genuinely able to lengthen his body by eleven inches, to levitate and float around a room near the ceiling, and to "play" an accordion without touching it. Home was one of the few mediums who allowed his seances to be conducted in full daylight, and was so concerned to quash the skeptics' dismissal of *all* mediums as frauds that he himself investigated and exposed a number of performers who were simply skilled conjurers taking advantage of popular interest in the phenomenon.

POST CARDS FROM THE BEYOND
– THE MEDIUM AS THE MESSENGER

THE SPECTACULAR physical phenomena of the nineteenth century seances can best be explained in terms of psychokinesis – that is, if one is willing to accept the extraordinary fact that people seem to be able to effect the movement of physical objects, or a change in composition of matter, simply with the force of thought. Many argue that modern physics supports this possibility, and research into psychokinesis continues. But although these wondrous spectacles are perhaps more appealing to the popular imagination, the real interest of the Spiritualist movement was the possibility of communicating with the spirits of the dead. According to Spiritualists, when a person dies his or her soul survives and can be contacted through a medium who serves as an intermediary between this world and the next. The doctrine of Spiritualism asserts that each human being has a "double" which is his or her "spirit" or "etheric" body. At death, the spirit leaves both the body and the earthly plane to reside in the spirit world. Those who have thus "passed over" retain their individual character and personality, and when they choose to appear to those they have left behind, they at first wear clothing resembling their usual mode of dress, which is replaced later on by a "spirit robe."

The spirit world consists of different layers closer to or farther away from the earth, depending upon the level of consciousness. The layer closest to the earth is inhabited by those who still have strong earthly attachments, and by those who are unaware of their condition. On one of the intermediate layers are the spirits who convey messages from friends and relatives who have gone even farther beyond. Those who have reached a higher level of consciousness go to more remote layers, blissful celestial spheres which are full of light and harmony.

All communication with the spirits takes place through a medium who, because of his or her special sensitivity or ability to go into trance, is uniquely available to these communications. Mediums are generally considered to fall into two categories – the first is the "mental" medium, who reveals information about the "sitter" who has come for a consultation. This information usually comes in the form of messages from dead friends and relatives of the sitter. The second category is that of the "physical medium" who, like Home, is able to produce extraordinary effects such as the movement of objects and even materializations. In Home's seances, for example, a disembodied hand would often appear, either to take up a pen and write a message or to go around the circle of attendees, jovially shaking hands with each of them. These "human" types of materializations are composed of a white substance called ectoplasm, and can sometimes take a form recognizable as a deceased relative or friend of one of the sitters at the seance. Other materializations that have mysteriously come forth in the presence of physical mediums have included bouquets of flowers and objects of jewelry.

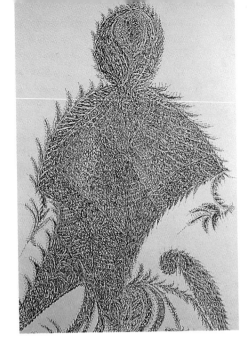

A medium generally works in one of the following ways:

1. Through clairvoyance, by "seeing" the spirits around the sitter, or through clairaudience, or "hearing" voices. The medium is in a waking state, and reports in a normal tone of voice what his or her impressions are.

2. By handling an article belonging to the sitter, or to the deceased with whom the sitter wants to communicate, and thereby being able to open up a channel through which messages can be received.

3. By going into a trance and giving messages through a new personality – their personal "control," or "spirit guide" – or by allowing the deceased to "take possession" and speak to the sitter directly. In these cases, the medium often takes on the voice and personality of the deceased relative.

4. Through "automatic writing" with the aid of a planchette or ouija board. A planchette is a small wooden board through which a pencil is inserted and that moves on casters in response to the guidance of a spirit. The ouija board enables the spirit to spell out messages with a pointer that moves in the direction of the letters of the alphabet, or towards the words "yes" and "no."

Physical mediums, on the other hand, operate through a variety of phenomena, some of which are designed only to prove the existence of spirits, and others which replace the verbal or written messages of mental mediums. These include:

1. "Table turning," or evidence that the spirit is present because he or she can cause a table to move in the seance. Sometimes this movement happens without any physical contact by the sitters or the medium, but in most cases all those present at the seance are resting their hands on top of the table.

2. Movement of other objects for the same purpose of proving that the spirits of the dead are present, and are using the medium's special powers to show that they still exist. Sometimes objects are coated with luminous paint to make them more visible in a darkened room.

3. Materialization of objects or creatures, called "apports," such as flowers, birds, stones or insects.

4. The production of ectoplasm, defined in *A Dictionary of Modern Spiritualism* as "A subtle living matter present in the physical body, primarily invisible but capable of assuming vaporous, liquid, or solid states and properties. It is extruded usually in the dark from the pores and various orifices of the body, and is slightly luminous, the more so when condensed. The temperature of the room is usually lowered when ectoplasm is produced; it possesses a characteristic smell and is cold to the touch..." This ectoplasm is believed to be the stuff used in the creation of human forms or parts of the body during a seance.

5. Voices which can be heard through trumpets or small megaphones, and are said to be those of the spirits wishing to communicate.

Most mediums nowadays are of the "mental" type rather than the "physical," and in fact much – though by no means all – of the physical phenomena of the nineteenth-century seance has been subsequently exposed as sometimes skillful and often ludicrously inept deception. For the authentic physical phenomena, and indeed for the striking accuracy of many of the messages delivered by mental mediums both past and present, a variety of explanations have been offered by contemporary researchers into the paranormal. To delve into these would lead us far off the track here. But perhaps it will suffice to say that, despite a thread of fraud and simple naivete running through the history of mediums and other "channels" and "seers," there is enough solid evidence to warrant being open to the possibility that a "beyond" of some sort does indeed exist, and that sometimes those who inhabit it appear to be trying to send us a post card.

VISITING A MEDIUM

For those who are particularly concerned with the authenticity of communications through mediums, Britain's Society for Psychical Research has prepared guidelines for those people who are intending to visit one. They suggest that certain precautions be taken to insure that one does not inadvertently provide information that can be fraudulently used by the medium. Their recommendations follow:

1

Make an anonymous booking for the sitting by telephone, or use another name.

2

Keep your belongings with you during the sitting so they cannot be used to provide the medium or a hidden assistant to provide clues.

3

Take into account how much your own behavior, facial expressions, appearance and dress can be a source of information for the medium. Try not to give away information in general conversation or in response to comments during the sitting itself — even a yes or no response to remarks can lead the medium towards structuring a message which

appears to come from another source, but it in fact has been given by the sitter.

4

Ask that a verbatim transcript be made, either by audiotaping or shorthand.

5

Consider the possibility of having someone sit in for you who has no information about the deceased person you wish to contact. This method, known as a "proxy sitting," eliminates all possibility that the medium will simply be "mirroring" your own knowledge or unconscious expectations back to you.

On the other hand, the Society recommends that the sitter remain open minded and presume that the spirit "communicator" is present and trying to convey his or her message under difficult circumstances. They caution against asking questions at a first sitting, as it might disrupt the flow of the communication. Persistent questioning or interrogation, arguing, contradicting and asserting your own opinions, or, conversely, being totally unresponsive, are likely to discourage the medium and cause the communication to be disrupted.

Finally, although this is not among the Society's recommendations, one might simply go for the fun of it – and, if the medium seems to be very insightful or delivers some astonishing news, be able to enjoy the fact that he or she has some extraordinary gift and is both willing and able to share it, whatever the actual source of the message might be.

GHOST STORIES

Ghost stories have always entertained and
intrigued us — and are sometimes impossible to
dismiss as mere imagination and fantasy.

SOME OF the earliest post cards from the beyond, it seems, must have come in the form of wandering spirits. Otherwise, so many cultures through the ages, in so many different parts of the world, would not have taken so much care to prevent these spirits from wandering into the world of the embodied and causing fright, disruption, or actual harm.

From the cave burials of Neanderthal man, where skeletons have been bound up in a way that has provoked some scholars to postulate an attempt to keep the corpse from wandering about, to the sophisticated mummification procedures developed in Egypt, one can find a widespread belief that both the preparation of the corpse and the ceremonies accompanying its disposal were of central importance in ensuring that its spirit was able to "rest easy" in the hereafter. In Egypt, the mummy was required both as resting place for the spirit in this world, and as vehicle for its use in the next. And, as in most ancient cultures, there was a powerful taboo against disturbing the resting places of the dead.

It is a taboo that survives today, of course, not only in tribal cultures relatively untouched by modern civilization, but also in our own. But, unlike our ancient forebears, we now seem to be

Many explanations have been offered for why some people seem to hang around as ghosts, including violent death or improper burial....

quite certain that the physical body, as it has been known to us while the person was alive, will be of no use to the departed. Remnants of ancient and primitive beliefs could be said to survive to the extent that physical burial is practiced rather than cremation. In this tradition, the corpse is dressed up in its "Sunday best," and sometimes buried with its favorite possessions. And some Oriental cultures still bury their dead with "money" to be used in the afterlife. But the more ancient practice of burying the dead with a complete travel kit of material possessions to be used in the hereafter has for the most part vanished along with the ancient cultures who believed such kits were necessary.

But one remnant of the ancient taboos and beliefs surrounding the spirits of the dead still lurks in the collective unconscious. The lineage of our persistent belief in ghosts, if we examine it closely, can be traced directly to the taboos and beliefs surrounding improper burial and sudden, violent death. There are countless examples of these in ancient cultures. In Mesopotamia, for example, anyone who had suffered a violent or unexplained death, who was not properly buried, or whose remains were disturbed, could return after death and haunt the burial grounds and ruined buildings. They might also take refuge in the mountains and deserts, where they could seize travelers and take them away. In early Christian Europe it was commonly believed that unless the dead were given the proper honor and ritual, their ghosts would return to take revenge or reclaim their property. And anyone who met an untimely death, such as a woman who died in childbirth, was a prime candidate to become a wandering spirit. Islamic folklore contains references to the fact that if a man was murdered the site of his death would be haunted, and one might even hear groans coming from his ghost. In some parts of India ceremonies are still held for the spirits of the dead to prevent them from becoming evil spirits, and those who have suffered a violent death are given special ceremonies to pre-

... Socrates speculated that those who are too attached to their bodies are unable to leave the earthly plane.

vent them from becoming "haunting ghosts."

Socrates offered another explanation for ghosts, essentially saying that if a soul is too focused on the body it will have trouble leaving it when the time comes. "The corporeal is heavy, oppressive, earthly and visible," he said. "So the soul which is tainted by its presence is weighed down and dragged back into the visible world, through fear (as they say) of Hades or the invisible, and hovers about tombs and graveyards. The shadowy apparitions which have actually been seen there are the ghosts of those souls which have not got clear away, but still retain some portion of the visible; which is why they can be seen."[2]

At the end of the first century, Pliny the Younger recounted a tale about the philosopher Athenodorus who was able to rent a house in Athens at a very cheap price because it was supposedly haunted. On the first night of his stay in his new home, Athenodorus was awakened by the sound of clanking chains. There, standing in front of him, was "the spectre of an old man, emaciated and filthy, with a long flowing beard and hair standing on end, wearing fetters on his legs and shaking the chains on his wrists." The old man beckoned to Athenodorus, who followed him into the courtyard. There, the ghost pointed wordlessly to a spot on the ground and promptly vanished. The next day Athenodorus informed the authorities, who arranged for the ground to be dug up in the appropriate spot. There they found a skeleton of a man with chains at his wrists and ankles. After the chains had been removed, and the skeleton had been buried properly, the ghost never returned.

Beliefs, superstitions, and legends aside, there are plenty of ghost stories with enough credibility to allow the possibility that at least some of those who depart their bodies don't quite find their way to a shore so distant that we can no longer see them. Perhaps one of the most

instructive cases is that of the haunting of the Crown Hotel in South Yorkshire.[3] The story goes like this:

One day, during the 1950s, a hotel employee saw a young woman pass through the foyer, making her way to the bar and then walking right through it. Some days later a hotel guest appeared at the cashier's desk, obviously in a state of agitation, insisting he was ready to check out even though he had been booked for a stay of several more days. Reluctant to talk at first, he was finally persuaded to explain the reasons for his early departure. It seems that he had awoken during the previous night, feeling the "presence of something" in his room. When he opened his eyes he saw a young woman standing at the foot of his bed. Curious to find out who she was, he got out of bed, walked towards her and reached out to touch her; his hand passed right through her. Her hair was in a bun, he said, and she was wearing a white high-necked blouse, a long black skirt, flat, black shoes and black stockings.

The man's description of the woman matched the description given by the hotel employee who had seen the apparition in the foyer. As it turned out, there had been a murder in the hotel shortly after the second world war. The chef of the hotel at that time was having an affair with a waitress who worked there, and one night they had quarreled. The chef had strangled the young woman, and later hanged himself in a part of the hotel which had subsequently been turned into guest rooms. Investigation of the story in old newspaper accounts not only confirmed that the murder had indeed taken place, but that the young woman's body had been found dressed in the same clothes she had been wearing as a ghost. The hotel management eventually brought in a medium, who managed to establish communication with the young woman's ghost. It seems she hadn't fully realized she was dead, and now that her situation has been made clear, she has disappeared from the hotel once and for all.

WITCHES AND WARLOCKS, SAINTS AND WANDERING SPIRITS

The night of October 31, which we now celebrate as Hallowe'en, grew out of a somewhat unlikely marriage of Christianity and the ancient Celtic traditions. October 31 was the last day of the Celtic year, and it was believed that witches and warlocks were abroad on that night. According to Scottish tradition those who are born on this day will have "second sight," or clairvoyant powers. With the arrival of Christianity, the night was transformed into "All Hallows Eve," the night before All Saints Day on November 1 when all the saints of the Catholic Church who don't have a special day of their own are celebrated. November 2, furthermore, is All Souls Day when the living pray for the souls of the dead. Thus a curious combination of fear and reverence, death and superstition, have been bound together in the popular imagination – and, it might be argued, remain so today.

He was unsedated, fully conscious and had a low temperature. He was a rather religious person and believed in life after death. We expected him to die, and he probably did too as he was asking us to pray for him. In the room where he was lying there was a staircase leading to the second floor. Suddenly he exclaimed, "See, the angels are coming down the stairs. The glass has fallen and broken." All of us in the room looked toward the staircase where a drinking glass had been placed on one of the steps. As we looked, we saw the glass break into a thousand pieces without any apparent cause. It did not fall, it simply exploded. The angels, of course, we did not see. A happy and peaceful expression came over the patient's face and the next moment he expired. Even after his death the serene, peaceful expression remained on his face.

From the book, *At the Hour of Death*

DEATHBED APPARITIONS

The dying often see spirits who have come to escort them to whatever awaits them in the afterlife. Often these apparitions are of relatives or friends who have already died.

THE APPEARANCE of an "angel of death" can be found as a theme in literature at least as far back as the Bible. Doctor Melvin Morse, whose studies of the near-death experiences of children will be explored later, quotes a study done by French historian Philippe Aries, documenting the fact that before about the year 1000, it was common for the dying to know when their time had come, to review their lives, their achievements and failures, and to ask the forgiveness of friends and family for any wrongs they felt they had done. As they approached closer to death, they would often speak to those around the deathbed about their visions of God, and of seeing friends and relatives who had died before them.

However, in the modern world of hospitals, intensive care units, high-tech life support systems, restricted visiting hours, and a general tendency to avoid death and the dying as much as possible, these "angels of death" seem to have all but disappeared. When they do appear, the response of medical staff is likely to be a prescription of drugs to deal with the "anxiety" or "hallucinations" of the dying patients, or at least to firmly discourage them from talking about it. Furthermore, the death of a relative is usually an event that takes place far from the center of a family household, and it requires a special effort on the part of both family and medical staff to ensure that the bed of one who is dying is surrounded by loving family and friends. It is likely,

*Popular folklore about the "angel of death" may
well come from the actual experiences of those who
were dying. Similarly, the image of a dying person
might appear to relatives at the time of death.*

though, that the "angels" have not disappeared, at least as far as the dying are concerned. It is just that most of the rest of us are not around to hear about their visits when they happen.

Like the near-death experience itself, some researchers have undertaken to investigate the visions of the dying, and to publish them. Among the first of these researchers in contemporary times was Sir William Barrett, whose *Death-Bed Visions*, published in 1926, is cited as a classic in its field. One of the most famous cases in the book was reported by Lady Barrett, who was herself a physician. She tells of a woman who lay dying after giving birth to a healthy baby, and who reported seeing a "lovely brightness" and spoke to her deceased father as though he were standing in the room. The dying woman was puzzled about one thing, however: What was her sister Vida doing there? In fact, Vida had died some three weeks before, but the news had been kept from the pregnant woman because of her frail condition.

Lady Barrett's patient may be one of the most startling deathbed visions on record, especially because it featured the appearance of a relative not known by the patient to be deceased, but there are countless other stories just as provocative. One of them is repeated in *True Ghost Stories*, compiled by Vivienne Rae-Ellis, and tells of two nurses working on the night shift in a hospital who saw a man dressed in a chauffeur's uniform coming out of the elevator. The man informed the nurses that he was coming to visit his wife, and they directed him to the women's ward. They did not see him return, and subsequent investigation suggested that he had mysteriously vanished on the way; no one else who would have been in a position to witness his passing managed to see him. The inquiry into his mysterious disappearance might never have gone any farther were it not for the fact that on following day, the nurses heard the story of a remarkable coincidence that had the nursing staff buzzing. A woman who had been in the hospital suffering from a terminal illness had died during the previous night – and on the very same day her husband, a chauffeur, had died in an automobile accident.

News of a similar kind of sighting, though within more conventional context, came from a nine-year-old girl who had entered the room of a dying grandmother who was being cared for in the family's home. After a few moments in the room, the girl emerged with a puzzled look on her face and said to her mother, "There are two grannies in the room. First I talked to granny, and then a lighted lady named Beth came and talked to me and granny. Then they left together."

Sometimes the visions seen by the dying appear to be frightening. This is in part culturally determined, but is probably most often related to the degree of acceptance reached by the individual ...

The mother went with the child back into the room and saw that indeed, the grandmother had died. She also knew something that the child had not known – the name the girl had used for the "lighted lady", Beth, was the name of the dying woman's own deceased mother, a great-grandmother who had died before the child was born.[4]

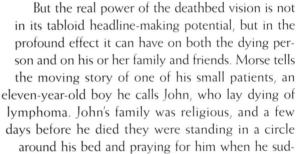

But the real power of the deathbed vision is not in its tabloid headline-making potential, but in the profound effect it can have on both the dying person and on his or her family and friends. Morse tells the moving story of one of his small patients, an eleven-year-old boy he calls John, who lay dying of lymphoma. John's family was religious, and a few days before he died they were standing in a circle around his bed and praying for him when he suddenly sat up and shouted "There are beautiful colors in the sky! There are beautiful colors and more colors. You can double jump up here, double jump!" By the following dawn, John's condition had worsened, but, Morse says, "John had more to communicate. Opening his eyes wide, he asked his grieving parents to 'let me go. Don't be afraid,' he said, 'I've seen God, angels and shepherds. I see the white horse.'" He told his family they mustn't feel sorry for him, because he had seen where he was going and it was beautiful. "John's family left the hospital knowing that they had done everything they could to save their son," concludes Morse. "They also firmly believed that he was safely at rest in God's hands."[5]

Karlis Osis and Erlunder Haraldsson published *At the Hour of Death*, their study of deathbed visions, in 1977. It was compiled from the responses thousands of questionnaires sent to medical personnel to gain information about people's behavior just prior to death, and specifically excluded those who seemed to be confused and disoriented, or who were heavily sedated at the time – as did Sir Barrett's study, by the way. In the overwhelming majority of cases, the visions reported were perceived by the dying patient as some kind of escort to the "other side," sometimes God or an angel, but more often deceased relatives. Many patients would converse with these otherworldly visitors just as if they were embodied people, and at the same time be able to speak to those physically present in the room with perfect clarity and calmness. The apparitions seemed to comfort most patients, although a few became frightened or appeared to argue against being "escorted" just now. And the visions were generally followed relatively quickly by the patient's death.

Occasionally, it seems, the escorts find they are no longer needed after all and eventually disappear. One of the people Moody interviewed in his study of near-death experiences had already met his escort during the initial stages of his encounter with death. He reported that as soon as he had left his body he found that he was attended by the presence of a friend named Bob who had recently died. In the way of so many people who have had such experiences, he gropes for words to describe his view of this friend's presence: "I could see him in my mind and felt like he was there, but it was strange. I didn't see him as his physical body. I could see things, but not in the physical form, yet just as clearly, his looks, everything. Does that make sense? He was there but he didn't have a physical body; it was kind of like a clear body, and I could sense every part of it.... I kept asking him, 'Bob, where do I go now? What has happened? Am I dead or not?' And he never answered me, never said a word." At various times during his recovery, Moody's subject would see his friend again in his hospital room. "And I would ask him again, 'What's going on?' but never any answer." Eventually, shortly after the man heard his doctors say he was going to live, Bob disappeared, never to return. "It was almost as if he were waiting until I passed that final frontier and then he would tell me," the man concludes. "[He] would give me the details on what was going on."[6]

Sometimes, the visions of the dying and their willingness to enter the luminous realm to which they are being beckoned must contend with the prayers and wishes of others to keep them in their bodies. Raymond Moody reports one such case in *Life After Life*, where a beloved

It seems that the prayers and wishes of a dying person's loved ones actually do have an effect, and can keep them from moving into a realm which they themselves perceive to be joyous and bright.

elderly aunt finally confronted her niece and asked her, in so many words, to tell the rest of the family to let her get on with her journey. "She looked at me and said, 'Joan, I have been over there, over to the beyond and it is beautiful over there. I want to stay, but I can't as long as you keep praying for me to stay with you. Your prayers are holding me over here. Please don't pray any more.' We did all stop," said the woman, "and shortly after that she died."

Melvin Morse tells the story of one small boy whose comatose condition prevented him from expressing his wishes, but who managed to find a unique way to ask a similar favor of his family. The boy was five years old, and dying of a brain tumor. Almost twenty-four hours a day during the three weeks he was in a coma, his family had surrounded his bedside praying for his recovery, taking time only briefly, and in shifts, to eat and rest. At the end of the third week, the pastor of the family's church came to the hospital. Obviously somewhat nonplussed, he said that he had a message to deliver. The pastor had had a dream, he said, in which the boy had appeared so vividly that it was "as though he was right there in the room, talking to me face to

Here, William Blake eloquently contrasts the joy
of the departing spirit with the sorrow of those
he is leaving behind.

face." In the dream, the boy said, "It's my time to die. You must tell my parents to quit praying. I am supposed to go now."

When the pastor had finished delivering his startling message, the boy's parents said one more prayer, touched their child's comatose body, and told him that although they would miss him, he had their permission to die. "Suddenly the boy regained consciousness," Morse reports. "He thanked his family for letting him go and told them he would be dying soon. He died the next day."[7]

Along with the visions of the dying, there are numerous accounts of relatives and friends seeing apparitions of those at the moment of death, or shortly thereafter. They are referred to as "crisis apparitions" by those who label such things, and in some cases may be seen by more than one person when they happen. A classic example of these not-uncommon occurrences is given in *Phantasms of the Living*, a collection of cases compiled by F.W.H. Myers, E. Gurney, and F. Podmore.

On the day of his unexpected death, a Methodist minister had awakened, had his breakfast and spent most of the day reading the Bible. Several times he had gone to the front gate, as if he was expecting someone to arrive, and seemed restless and distracted. He later began to talk about his son, from whom he had been estranged, and said he hoped that would soon be set on the right path in life. The minister's death occurred completely unexpectedly at about a quarter to seven in the evening.

Meanwhile, hours away, the estranged son had no idea of his father's death. His account of what happened was carefully recorded by investigators of the story, as follows: "My little son, Arthur, who was then five years old, and the pet of his grandpa, was playing on the floor, when I entered the house at a quarter to seven o'clock, Friday evening, July 11th, 1879. I was very tired, having been receiving and paying for staves all day, and it being an exceedingly sultry evening, I lay down by Artie on the carpet, and entered into conversation with my wife – not, however, in regard to my parents. Artie, as usually was the case, came and lay down with his little head upon my left arm, when all at once he exclaimed, 'Papa! Papa! Grandpa!' I cast my eyes towards the ceiling, or opened my eyes, I am not sure which, when, between me and the joists (it was an old-fashioned log cabin), I saw the face of my father as plainly as ever I saw him in my life. He appeared to me to be very pale, and looked sad, as I had seen him upon my last visit to him three months previous. I immediately spoke to my wife, who was sitting within a few feet of me, and said, 'Clara, there is something wrong at home; my father is either dead or very sick.' She tried to persuade me that it was my imagination, but I could not help feeling that something was wrong. Being very tired, we soon after retired, and about ten o'clock Artie woke me up repeating, 'Papa, grandpa is here'... Next morning I expressed my determination to go at once to Indianapolis. My wife made light of it and overper-suaded me, and I did not go until Monday morning, and upon arriving at home (my father's), I found that he had been buried the day before, Sunday, July 13th."

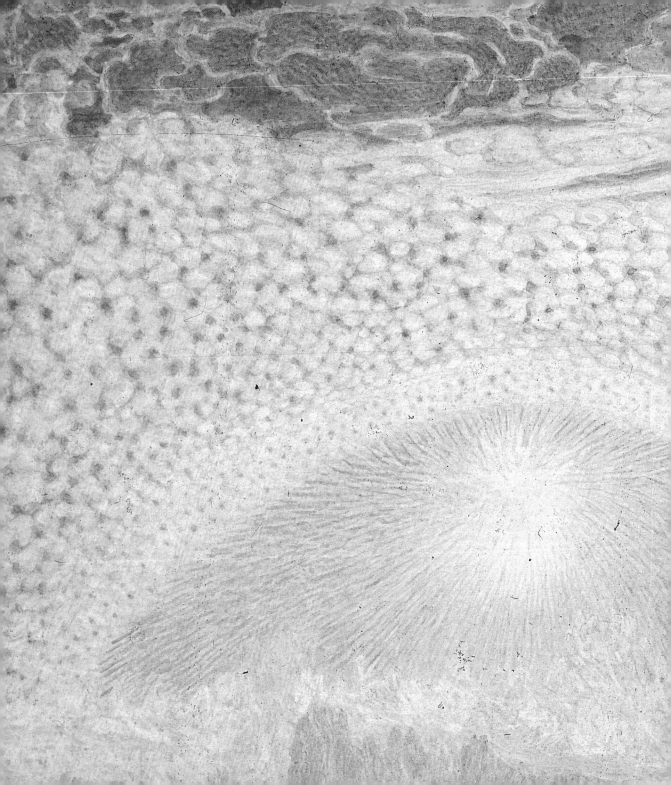

4

TRUE DEATH
ADVENTURES

He came back to life and suddenly sat up — those weeping around the body were very upset and ran away. "I was guided by a handsome man in a shining robe," he said. "When we reached the top of a wall, there was a wide and pleasant meadow, with light flooding in that seemed brighter than daylight or the midday sun. I was very reluctant to leave, for I was enraptured by the place's pleasantness and beauty and by the company I saw there. From now on I must live in a completely different way."

Adapted from *A History of the English Church and People* by the Venerable Bede

At first, when the light came, I wasn't sure what was happening, but then it asked, it kind of asked me if I was ready to die. It was like talking to a person, but a person wasn't there. The light's what was talking to me, but in a voice. Now, I think that the voice... actually realized that I wasn't ready to die. You know, it was just kind of testing me more than anything else. Yet, from the moment the light spoke to me, I felt really good — secure and loved. The love which came from it is just unimaginable, indescribable. It was a fun person to be with! And it had a sense of humor, too — definitely!

Experience reported in Raymond Moody's *Life After Life*

MOVING TOWARD THE LIGHT

THE IMAGERY found in the Christian medieval journeys to death and back differs in many ways from contemporary accounts of near-death experiences. Some of these differences must be attributed to priestly intervention in the stories to serve their own purposes. For example one traveler, in a story originally circulated by the head of a Cistercian monastery, reports that of all the beings he saw in heaven, the Cistercians were clearly the most luminous! Other differences are traceable to the profound changes in culture and society that have taken place over the centuries.

Today's near-death travelers are somewhat more likely to find themselves being guided toward the other world by deceased family members than by an angel complete with wings and halo, and the "bridge" common to the medieval journey is now much more likely to be a gigantic culvert, or a tunnel that calls to mind the imagery used in today's discussions of theoretical vacuums or "wormholes" that would allow us to travel faster than the speed of light to other universes. In *Otherworld Journeys*, author Carol Zaleski points out that the bridge in medieval times was almost as magical a thing as the theoretical time-travel tunnels through space seem to most of us in this century. In the earliest days of their construction these marvelous structures crossing rivers were regarded with something approaching superstitious awe, which was reinforced by the fact that their maintenance was often delegated to monastic orders whose pious attentions presumably kept them from tumbling down due to the sheer impossibility of their existence.

Cultural differences aside, though, the experiences of those who have clinically "died" and subsequently revived have a number of features in common, no matter what the individual imaginative differences might be. A woman in India may find herself riding a "spangled cow" to the realm of light, while a busy New York professional finds herself hailing a taxi, but they both end up in a place that is recognizably the same. Not all people experience all aspects of what has been so carefully defined as the near-death experience, but enough of them experience the same sorts of things that we are forced to acknowledge that the phenomenon has earned the right to its own acronym, the "NDE."

Raymond Moody, the contemporary pioneer of near-death research, has described the near-death experience like this:

"A man is dying and, as he reaches the point of greatest physical distress, he hears himself pronounced dead by his doctor. He begins to hear an uncomfortable noise, a loud ringing or buzzing, and at the same time feels himself moving very rapidly through a long dark tunnel. After this, he suddenly finds himself outside of his own physical body, but still in the immediate physical environment, and he sees his own body from a distance, as though he is a spectator. He watches the resuscitation attempt from this unusual vantage point and is in a state of emotional upheaval.

"After a while, he collects himself and becomes more accustomed to his odd condition. He notices that he still has a 'body,' but one of a very different nature and with very different powers from the physical body he has left behind. Soon other things begin to happen. Others come to meet and to help him. He glimpses the spirits of relatives and friends who have already died, and a loving, warm spirit of a kind he has never encountered before – a being of light – appears before him. This being asks him a question, nonverbally, to make him evaluate his life and helps him along by showing him a panoramic, instantaneous playback of the major events of his life. At some point he finds himself approaching some sort of barrier or border, apparently representing the limit between earthly life and the next life. Yet, he finds that he must go back to the earth, that the time for his death has not yet come. At this point, he resists, for by now he is taken up with his experiences in the afterlife and does not want to return. He is overwhelmed by intense feelings of joy, love, and peace. Despite his attitude, though, he somehow reunites with his physical body and lives. Later he tries to tell others, but he has trouble doing so. In the first place, he can find no human words adequate to describe these unearthly episodes. He also finds that others scoff, so he stops telling other people. Still, the experience affects his life profoundly, especially his views about death and its relationship to life." [from Raymond A. Moody, Jr., M.D., *Life After Life.*]

As Moody himself points out, it is rare that a person actually goes through every step in the experience as he describes it. Rather, his description is a kind of compilation of the most common events. In the following pages we will look primarily at these common ingredients, though

Virtually all those who have been through a near-death experience stress that ordinary language is utterly inadequate to express what they have seen and felt.

some variations on the theme will also be examined. Before we embark on the journey, it will be good to take note of a few details concerning the map.

The first of these concern the specific experiences which have been determined to constitute the typical "near death experience." Raymond Moody is credited with being the first to enumerate these events, or characteristics, and his book *Life After Life* is essential reading for anyone who is genuinely interested in the subject. Moody's work was followed by that of Kenneth Ring, whose more rigorous scientific approach has been appreciated by all those who are not only genuinely but also "seriously" interested in the subject, including Moody himself. In the past decade, both Moody and Ring, along with dozens of other researchers, have further elaborated and refined definitions of the near-death experience – most of them with only slight variations on the original. The most notable of these efforts, along with a complete listing of the works of Moody and Ring, is to be found in the bibliography and further reading lists. For our purposes here, some of these discrete characteristics and events have been combined under larger headings.

Second, the intent of this presentation is more to facilitate an unveiling the mysteries of the near-death experience than it is to discuss the pros and cons of accepting the experience as "real." The details of an experiencer's medical condition, or even the person's gender, will be brought in only when it seems particularly relevant to the experience, and debates about possible physiological explanations for this or that phenomenon have been left to others more qualified to participate in them.

Third, the "ineffability" of the experience is one which Raymond Moody stresses in his groundbreaking work. For this reason, the firsthand reports of various stages of the near-death journey have been left whenever possible in their original, often inarticulate and groping form. These unedited statements say more about "ineffability" than volumes of polished commentary could ever hope to say.

Finally, it is always good to admit one's prejudices when starting out on a journey. In this case, the prejudice is that the experiences of those who have "died" and been "reborn" – no matter what the physical cause or circumstances of the event – have something to tell us all about the spiritual content and meaning of our lives. With this admission of prejudice in mind, then, it is time to take off our shoes and start the journey. We are about to enter sacred ground.

That's what meditation is: to see your body-and-mind complex without getting identified with it. Then suddenly a new center starts integrating in you. By using it you create it, by using it more, you intensify it. And soon a totally different phenomenon is experienced: the existence of the soul. Then you know that birth was not your beginning, you existed before — and then death is not going to be the end, you will exist afterwards.

Osho, *Sermons in Stones*

I was more conscious of my mind at the time than of that physical body.... And before, all my life, it had been exactly reversed. The body was my main interest and what was going on in my mind, well, it was just going on, and that's all. But after this happened, my mind was the main point of attraction, and the body was second — it was only something to encase my mind. I didn't care if I had a body or not. It didn't matter because for all I cared my mind was what was important.

Life After Life

THE SEPARATION

During the early stages of apparent death, many people discover themselves viewing their surroundings — and their own bodies — from a perspective outside their physical form.

IT WOULD be easy to misunderstand the depth of the above statement from *Life After Life* if one took the word "mind" to mean the ceaseless buzz of thoughts about the past, the future, and what's on the menu for dinner tonight, that most of us live with every day. And perhaps the statement would not truly be representative of

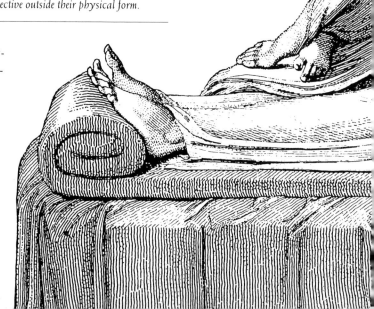

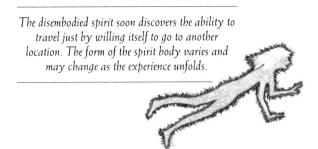

The disembodied spirit soon discovers the ability to travel just by willing itself to go to another location. The form of the spirit body varies and may change as the experience unfolds.

such depth had it not been offered in the context of how the woman in question felt her subsequent life had been transformed by her experience. She was offering it by way of explanation for a deeper and more lasting change, a shift in "identification" if you will, from the transient, mortal body toward the transcendent, immortal "soul."

In the West, we suffer from a certain poverty of language in describing states of consciousness so uncommon we consider them to be "altered." If, instead of the word "mind," we substitute Patanjali's "Perceiver" or even more simply, the word "consciousness," we can get somewhat closer to understanding the condition that those who have been separated from their bodies are trying to describe.

This separation – commonly known as an "out-of-body experience" or "OBE" – often takes place as the first stage of the near-death experience. It can be confusing or even frightening at first – people suddenly find that they are somehow outside their own physical bodies, looking from that vantage point at themselves and those around them. The experience is so strange that they sometimes at first don't even recognize the physical body, obviously in some kind of crisis, as their own. When they do finally recognize themselves, they don't know what to do with this extraordinary information: "I thought I was dead, and I wasn't sorry that I was dead, but I just couldn't figure out where I was supposed to go. My thought and my consciousness were just like they are in life, but I just couldn't figure all this out. I kept thinking, 'Where am I going to go? What am I going to do?' and 'My God, I'm dead! I can't believe it!' Because you never really believe, I don't think, fully, that you're going to die. It's always something that's going to happen to the other person, and although you know it you really never believe it deep down.... And so I decided I was just going to wait until all the excitement died down and they carried my body away, and try to see if I could figure out where to go from there."[1]

Others might actually try to communicate with medical personnel or bystanders from their disembodied state before realizing that the place they now reside is as insubstantial as the air itself. For example, one woman found herself standing next to the stretcher where her body lay, in the midst of a frantic medical team trying to restart her heart: "The doctors and nurses were pounding on my body, to try to get IV's started, and to get me back, and I kept trying to tell them, 'Leave me alone. All I want is to be left alone. Quit pounding on me.' But they didn't hear me. So I tried to move their hands to keep them from beating on my body, but nothing would happen. I couldn't get anywhere.'"[2] It is partly because of the detailed descriptions of resuscitation efforts subsequently given by these patients that physicians have been forced to examine some of their most cherished assumptions about how human beings are actually put together. But, not surprisingly, most people are so confused by their unfamiliar state that they don't take the time to notice the details.

"People were walking up from all directions to get to the wreck," says one accident victim. "I could see them, and I was in the middle of a very narrow walkway. Anyway, as they came by they wouldn't seem to notice me. They would just keep walking with their eyes straight ahead. As they came real close, I would try to turn around, to get out of their way, but they would just walk *through* me."[3] It appears to be most often the case that it is only when people come to some kind of realization of their actual condition, or hear someone present declaring them to be dead, that the next step on their journey is taken.

In many cases, however, they first have an opportunity to discover that in their disembodied state they can travel in unaccustomed ways. "There was a lot of action going on, and people running around the ambulance," says another accident victim. "And whenever I would look at a person to wonder what they were thinking, it was like a zoom-up, and I was there. But it seemed that part of me – I'll call it my mind – was still where I had been, several yards away from my body. When I wanted to see someone at a distance, it seemed like part of me, kind of like a tracer, would go to that person. And it seemed to me at the time that if something happened anyplace in the world that I could just be there."[4] Others get a preview of the telepathic form of communication they will be experiencing in the world to come: "I could see people all around, and I could understand what they were saying. I didn't hear them, audibly, like I'm hearing you. It was more like knowing what they were thinking, exactly what they were thinking, but only in my mind, not in their actual vocabulary. I would catch it the second before they opened their mouths to speak."[5]

*According to universal tradition, the original earthly Paradise and the still-existent otherworldly
Paradise were at first united, or in any case were in close proximity and communication. The means
of connection is described variously in different cultures — most vividly, perhaps, as a rainbow.*

Richard Heinberg, *Memories and Visions of Paradise*

*As Amr lay on his deathbed, a friend said to him, "You have often remarked that you would like to
find an intelligent man at the point of death and to ask him what his feelings were. Now I ask you
that question." Amr replied, "I feel as if heaven lay close upon the earth, and I between the two,
breathing through the eye of a needle."*

Amr Ibn Al-As, the conqueror of Egypt, died in 664
Quoted in *The Oxford Book of Death*, edited by D.J. Enright

THE RAINBOW BRIDGE

*The imagery in this painting of Jacob's dream by
Blake is echoed by many who struggle to find
words to express the journeys they have undertaken
during their near-death experiences.*

WE HAVE referred earlier to the fact that the method of travel away from the scene occu-
pied by the lifeless body and toward the "other world" can vary. Jacob's ladder to heav-
en can be found here, as well as Charon's river. One woman even wears an umbrella charm on a
chain today, as a reminder of her experience. "I went up and faded into a deep sliver-blue surrounding," she explains. Then came something that looked like a big umbrella without a stick.
This umbrella seemed to fold around me, and everything became very dark." It was in the safety
of her "umbrella" that she made her journey to the light beyond.

A water crossing was made by a woman dying of a post-partum hemorrhage: "On the distant shore, I could see all my loved ones who had died — my mother, my father, my sister, and
others.... They seemed to be beckoning me to come on over, and all the while I was saying, 'No,
no, I'm not ready to join you. I don't want to die. I'm not ready to go.'"[6] In the case of this reluctant traveler, she reports that she could simultaneously see what was happening in the hospital
room where her body lay. Her ferryboat turned around at the last moment, and she found herself back in her body.

An image of the rainbow comes into a report from a girl who, as a teenager, suffered a prolonged cardiac arrest as a result of an experiment with crack cocaine gone wrong. And, interestingly, some aspects of her journey call to mind the story told by Plato in his *Republic*, of the soldier Er's visit to the plains of Lethe. Or, even, some images of the Christian visits to purgatory, but without their explicitly fearful connotations. The girl had been watching the doctors try to restart her heart when she suddenly found herself inside a room filled with all her friends. "The room was very large and open at the top. It was like looking out at the sky. Sparks would fill the air and streaks of light zoomed up from the earth and burst into rainbows. I wanted very much to be one of those sparks, but I didn't know how to lift myself up and become one." The girl explains that there was a door in the room which, she knew, if she went through she would not be able to return. "I was afraid of the door but wanted to go through it too, if you know what I mean," she says. In the end, her deceased grandfather came along and told her she had to go back to her body, she had work to do.[7]

By far the majority of reports, though, speak of travel through something like a "tunnel." It is most commonly vast, but it may be as snug as a birth canal, and it is most commonly dark, but it may be luminous and feature multicolored streaks of light, just like a rainbow. Kenneth Ring began to ask his subjects if they had any sense of how fast they were traveling and the majority of those whose experience has included any sense of "speed" said they seemed to be traveling "faster than the speed of light," towards a destination far beyond the stars. Some people, among them those who have had some of the "deepest" experiences, or what Kenneth Ring calls the "core experience," have perhaps traveled so fast that they had no sense of "traveling" at all, and found themselves immediately in the light.

To comprehend and to understand God above all similitudes, as he is in himself, is to be God with God, without intermediary. (But) whoever wishes to understand this must have died to himself, and must live in God, and must run his gaze to the eternal Light in the ground of his spirit, where the hidden truth reveals itself without means. This brightness is so great that the loving contemplative, in his ground wherein he rests, sees and feels nothing but an incomprehensible Light; and through that simple Nudity which enfolds all things, he finds himself, and feels himself, to be that same Light by which he sees, and nothing else.

The Blessed Jan Van Ruysbroeck (1293-1381)

This light is not just a brilliance from whatever is at the end of the tunnel – it's an extremely *brilliant light. It's pure white. It's just so brilliant...this most magnificent, just gorgeous, beautiful, bright, white or blue-white light. It is so bright, it is brighter than a light that would immediately blind you, but this absolutely does not hurt your eyes at all. It is so bright, so brilliant, and so beautiful, but it doesn't hurt your eyes.*

From *Heading for Omega*

BRIGHTER THAN THE SUN

The light at the end
of the tunnel may be perceived as
a "being" of some kind,
or merely a "presence."

I**T IS WORTH** noting here that one of the standard questions Ring asks his subjects is whether the light they perceive at the end of the tunnel "hurts their eyes." One has the impression, reading through most accounts of the near-death experience, that it would not otherwise occur to anyone even to mention the possibility that the light could hurt their eyes. It may be pink instead of white, or glow with an orangey-gold quality. But what those who have seen it up close do report, almost without exception, is its otherworldly brilliance, and that it has a quality unlike anything they have ever seen on earth.

The light often appears at first as a glow at the end of a tunnel – "I heard the doctors say that I was dead, and that's when I began to feel as though I were tumbling, actually kind of floating,

150

through this blackness, which was some kind of enclosure. There are not really words to describe this. Everything was very black, except that, way off from me, I could see this light. It was a very, very brilliant light, but not too large at first. It grew larger as I came nearer and nearer to it."[8]

The sight of the light almost always brings a sense if "rightness" and peace to the traveler – "As I turned to face the light with my full 'body,' I felt happier than I ever had before or have since." It also seems to bring a certainty that it represents one's destination – and some people, with this knowledge, have been turned back before they reach it.

One woman got close enough to perceive the light as some sort of "being," though she couldn't tell whether it was a man or woman, or even whether that was relevant. At the point when she began to perceive the light more clearly, she says, it appeared to be a man. "I knew that everything would be all right, and I wanted to keep going toward him." But she heard her deceased mother's voice telling her to go back, and so she did. Another traveler tells his story with some amusement, relating how he traveled down a tunnel that seemed to fit him as snugly as a glove. He was moving through this tunnel when "I looked up and saw a beautiful, polished door, with no knob. Around the edges of the door I could see a really brilliant light, with rays just streaming like everybody was so happy in there, and reeling around, moving around. It seemed like it was awfully busy in there. I looked up and said, 'Lord, here I am. If you want me, take me.' Boy, he shot me back so fast it felt like I almost lost my breath!"[9]

The Lord of Love, omnipresent, dwelling in the heart of every living creature, all mercy, turns every face to himself. He is the supreme Lord, who through his grace moves us to seek him in our own hearts. He is the light that shines forever. He is the inner Self of all, hidden like a little flame in the heart. Only by the stilled mind can he be known. Those who realize him become immortal.

Shvetashvatara Upanishad

The light communicates to you and for the first time in your life...is a feeling of true, pure love. It can't be compared to the love of your wife, the love of your children, or some people consider a very intense sexual experience as love, and consider [it] possibly the most beautiful moment in their life — and it couldn't even begin to compare. All of these wonderful, wonderful feelings combined could not possibly compare to the feeling of true love. If you can imagine what pure love would be, this would be the feeling that you'd get from this brilliant white light.

Heading Towards Omega

THE HOMECOMING

Near-death experiencers may report meeting luminous escorts or guides during their journeys towards an overwhelmingly brilliant light.

I F IT IS DIFFICULT to describe the light in ordinary words, it seems to be all but impossible to describe the feeling of contact with this light when it happens. "It's almost like a person. It is not a person, but it is a being of some kind," in the words of one man who struggles to express it. "It is a mass of energy. It doesn't have a character like you would describe another *person*, but it has a character in that it is more than a just a *thing*. It is something to communicate to and acknowledge. And also in size, it just covers the entire vista before you. And it totally engulfs whatever the horizon might be."[10]

Of all the different stages of the journey, this is the one which perhaps most deeply transforms the lives of those who have been near death. In the presence of this "light" they have felt, or perhaps more accurately *become one with*, an overwhelming strength, tenderness and compassion which has transformed the way they view their own lives afterwards. Time after time, their attempts to speak about it reflect the fact that there are no words in ordinary language adequate to convey the experience of this light and the events that take place in its presence or under its

152

All the near-death travelers who have experienced being in the presence of the ineffable light have been awed by the overwhelming sense of love and acceptance emanating from it.

guidance. It is as if all the words we are accustomed to have become tattered from use, and as such are woefully inadequate to describe this luminous perfection of being. But people have tried, and the immediacy and sincerity of their efforts is more eloquent than any further commentary could be.

"It was a giant, infinite world of calm, and love, and energy and beauty. It was as though human life was unimportant compared to this. And yet it urged the importance of life at the same time it solicited death as a means to a better, different life. It was all being, all beauty, all meaning for existence. It was all the energy of the universe forever in one immensurable place."[11]

"There was the warmest, most wonderful love.... I felt light-good-happy-joy-at ease. Forever – eternal love. Time meant nothing. Just being. Love. Pure love. Love. The light was yellow. It was in, around, and through everything... it is God made visible. In, around, and through everything. One who has not experienced it cannot know its feeling. One who has experienced it can never forget it, yearns for its perfection, and longs for the embodiment of it."[12]

"I knew it was God. I knew...this is the hard part.... There is no doubt in my mind that it was God. God was me and I was God. I was part of the light and I was one with it. I was not separate. I am not saying that I am a supreme being. I was God, as you are, as everyone is."[13]

"Immediately, being a Christian, I had connected the light with Christ, who said, 'I am the light of the world.' I said to myself, 'If this is it, if I am to die, then I know who waits for me at the end, there in that light.'"[14]

"Peace. Homecoming. It's strange, because I never really verbalized that before. It was really like a homecoming. It was beautiful, it was magnificent. And it was so warm...another [kind of] warmth. An acceptance, a real acceptance."[15]

"At that point, I had no consciousness anymore of having a body. It was just pure consciousness. And this enormously bright light seemed almost to cradle me. I just seemed to exist in it and be part of it and be nurtured by it and the feeling just became more and more and more ecstatic and glorious and perfect. And everything about it was – if you took the one thousand best things that ever happened to you in your life and multiplied by a million, maybe you could get close to this feeling, I don't know. But you're just engulfed by it and you begin to know a lot of things...."[16]

You realize that you are suddenly in communication with absolute, total knowledge. It's hard to describe.... You can think of a question...and immediately know the answer to it. As simple as that.

Life After Life

To him who, purified, would break this vicious round
And breathe once more the air of heaven — greeting!
There in the courts of Hades wilt thou find
Leftward a beckoning cypress, tall and bright
From out whose root doth flow the water of Oblivion
Approach it not: guard thou thy thirst awhile.
For on the other hand — and further — wells
From bottomless pools the limpid stream of Memory,
Cool, full of refreshment. To its guardians cry thus:
"I am the child of earth and starry sky:
Know that I too am heavenly — but parched!
I perish: given then and quickly that clear draught
Of ice-cold Memory!" And from that fountainhead divine
Straightway they'll give thee drink quaffing the which
Thou with the other heroes eternally shalt rule.

Golden tablet found in an Orphic tomb

THE REMEMBRANCE

THE MESSAGE of the importance of love is one that those who return from death bring back with them; the other is of the importance of "knowledge," or "knowing," a recognition of the vast world of understanding that is available to us as human beings. In the East, these two "paths to God" are often distinguished as unique and recognizable, and describe different characteristics of the persons who are likely to be attracted to one or the other. It is also said that the two paths meet on the boundary of the transcendent: from following the path of meditation the capacity for love arises, and from love, the capacity for meditation or "knowing."

The knowledge and understanding gained in the presence of the "being of light" is transmitted directly, without need for verbalization. "It seemed whole Truths revealed themselves to

"Consciousness is life, says one woman who died
and then came back. "We will live in and through
much, but this consciousness... will continue."

me," says one woman. "Waves of thought – ideas greater and purer than I had ever tried to figure out came to me. Thoughts, clear without effort revealed themselves in total wholeness, although not in logical sequence. I, of course, being in that magnificent Presence, understood it all. I realized that consciousness is life. We will live in and through much, but this consciousness we know, that is behind our personality, will continue."[17]

Others may be in the process of exploring their surroundings in the luminous otherworld when they come across beautiful structures, "cities of light" that they intuitively know contain all the knowledge and understanding in the world. One woman who was prevented at the last moment from entering one of these cities wept as she recounted how much she had wanted to go on. "I could hear languages, all languages. Languages that I had never heard before and I could understand them. I wanted to be allowed to go on. I knew there was much more there and I wanted to be able to experience it, to see it.... There was the knowledge that was beyond anything that I could possibly try to describe to you. I began to realize that I was going to have to leave and I didn't want to leave."[18]

The revelations of others may be less detailed, but are no less profound. "When I floated out of my body and saw myself," says one black teenager from the East St. Louis projects who had drowned when he was about ten years old, "suddenly I realized that we are all the same. There ain't no black and there ain't no white. I saw that bright light and I knew it was all the colors there were, everything was in that light."[19] James, as he is named by Melvin Morse, was considered by his mother and the few other people he had told about his experience to be "talking trash" until a sympathetic and knowledgeable teacher heard his story and referred him to Morse. To be taken seriously, and to have a name to put on his extraordinary experience, was a tremendous relief for James. In the meantime, what he had seen had kept him in school,

157

committed to his studies, and away from the gangs that plagued his neighborhood. "I know that I am different," he admits. "I don't think about putting people down for fun like I used to.... I see life the way it really is. It is not meant to be played with."

Although we may understand many things on the "other side," it seems that we are not allowed to remember all of them when we return. Jayne Smith, who gave the following account, was speaking in public, and so her words have an anecdotal quality appropriate to the forum in which they were delivered. But she describes an experience common to many, and, appropriately, previews the subject of the following section. She describes her encounter with one of several luminous beings she met on her journey, "speaking" to him first with the following greeting:

"I know what's happened, I know that I've died."

And he said, "Yes, but you aren't going to be staying because it isn't time for you yet." And I said to him, "This is all so beautiful, this is all so perfect, what about my sins?"

And he said to me, "There are no sins. Not in the way you think about them on earth. The only thing that matters is how you think."

"What is in your heart?" he asked me. And somehow I immediately was able to look into my heart and I saw that there was nothing in my heart except love. And I understood exactly what he meant. And I said to him, "Of course." And I felt it was something I had always known and somehow I'd forgotten it until he'd reminded me of it. "Of course!"

And then I asked him, "Since I can't stay, since I'm going to be going back, I've another question to ask. Can you tell me – what's it all about?" [The audience laughs, and she joins in the laughter, explaining that she wanted to know how "the whole thing" worked.]

And he did tell me. And it only took two or three sentences. It was a very short explanation, and I understood it perfectly. And I said again, "Of course!" and again, I knew it was something I had always known and managed to forget."

And so I asked him, "Can I take all this back with me? There's so many people I want to tell all this to."

And he said, "You can take the answer to your first question" – which was the one about sin – but, he said, "the answer to the second question you won't be able to remember."[20]

All mankind is of one author, and is one volume; when one man dies, one chapter is not torn out of the book, but translated into a better language. And every chapter must be so translated. God employs several translators; some pieces are translated by age, some by sickness, some by war, some by justice, but God's hand is in every translation, and his hand shall bind up all our scattered leaves again for that library where every book shall lie open to one another.

John Donne, *Devotions*

I had the feeling that the closer this light got to me, the more awesome and the more pure this love — this feeling that I would call love... And this person said, "Do you know where you are?" I never got a chance to answer that question, for all of a sudden — quote, unquote — "my life passed before me."

Heading Toward Omega

JUDGMENT DAY

Virtually all those who have undergone the "life review" phase of the near-death experience report that this review takes place in an atmosphere not of condemnation but of love and forgiveness.

S O – *what about our sins?* Where are all the scales of judgment, the wrathful demons, the tormenting fires and thundering condemnations? Could they have been all in our own minds all along? Did we just *make them up?*

"You are shown your life – and you do the judging. Had you done what you should do? You think, 'Oh, I gave six dollars to someone that didn't have much, and that was great of me.' That didn't mean a thing. It's the little things – maybe a hurt child that you helped, or just to stop and say hello to a shut-in. Those are the things that are most important.... *You are judging yourself.* You have been forgiven all your sins, but are you able to forgive yourself for not doing the things you should have done, and some cheaty things that maybe you've done in your life? *Can you forgive yourself?* This is the judgment."[21] [italics added]

Kenneth Ring relates the story of one young man he calls "Hank," who was badly injured in an automobile accident when he was nineteen years old. His description of this phase of his

Even the most minute details of a person's life may be re-experienced during the life review. But the purpose seems to be primarily that of teaching the individual about the importance of love.

near-death experience calls to mind the biblical "Book of Life" or the Tibetan "Akashic Records" and suggests there is a real, experiential basis for the many mythologies which assert that even the tiniest of deeds in life do not go unnoticed by the Whole. Hank found himself in a large room with a number of luminous beings when another, "brighter" being entered the room and approached him. "Do you know where you are?" Hank was asked. When he answered in the affirmative, the response was "What is your decision?"

"When he said that," says Hank, "it was like I knew everything that was stored in my brain. Everything I'd ever known from the beginning of my life I immediately knew about. And also, what was kind of scary was that I knew everybody else in the room knew I knew, and that there was no hiding anything – the good times, the bad times, everything.... I had a total, complete, clear knowledge of everything that had ever happened in my life – even little minute things."

Hank came out of this review with a completely new understanding of what was important in life: "I realized that there are things that every person is sent to earth to realize and to learn. For instance, to share more love, to be more loving toward one another. To discover that the most important thing is human relationships and love, and not materialistic things. And to realize that every single thing that you do in your life is recorded and that even though you pass by it not thinking at the time, it always comes up later."[22]

What has come to be called the "life review" stage of the near-death experience might best be described as the place where the path of love and the path of understanding meet. The events of one's life become clear for the first time in the context of a transcendent understanding of what is truly significant and what is mere posturing, what is acquired and superficial morality, and what is true love and caring. "What is in your heart?" we are asked, and even though it might be painful to see the many ways in which we have betrayed our own hearts, or wounded the hearts of others, we nevertheless are invited to forgive ourselves and to learn from our mistakes.

"What occurred was, every emotion I have ever felt in my life, I felt. And my eyes were showing me the basis of how that emotion affected my life. What my life had done so far to affect other people's lives using the feeling of pure love that was surrounding me as the point of comparison.... Looking at yourself from the point of how much love you have spread to other

*The life review usually includes both
a panoramic playback of events and an intimate
and immediate understanding of the effects of one's
actions on others.*

people is devastating. You will never get over it. I am six years away from that day, and I am not over it yet."[23] The same person who reported this experience of the "life review" was then taken to one of the beautiful cities that features in some accounts, and entered a cathedral-like building: "Now, this cathedral was literally built of knowledge. This was a place of learning I had come to. I could sense it."

Not a single report mentions even a distant echo of our common earthly tendency to make excuses for our thoughtlessness, to find someone else to blame for our sufferings, or to try to justify ourselves in others' eyes. In the "judgment day" of the hereafter there seems to be neither tribunal nor need for a defense. In any case the "Truth" of the matter is, obviously, both apparent and accessible to everybody concerned: "This communication is what you might call telepathic. It's absolutely instant, absolutely clear. It wouldn't even matter if a different language was being spoken...whatever you thought and attempted to speak, it would be instant and absolutely clear. There would never be a doubtful statement made."[24]

It could be frightening to know with such certainty that one was so transparent, that there was no possibility of covering up any of the things we might normally prefer to hide. But the pervasive quality of acceptance and love seems to make such familiar concerns irrelevant: "When the light appeared, the first thing he said to me was "What do you have to show me that you've done with your life?" or something to that effect. And that's when these flashbacks started...'I knew that [the being of light] was there with me the whole time, that he carried me back through the flashbacks, because I felt his presence and because he made comments here and there. He was trying to show me something in each one of these flashbacks. It's not like he was trying to see what I had done – he knew already – but he was picking out these certain flashbacks of my life and putting them in front of me so that I would have to recall them. All through this, he kept stressing the importance of love.... There wasn't any accusation in any of this, though. When he came across times when I had been selfish, his attitude was only that I had been learning from [these actions] too."[25]

Or, as another person said, so eloquently and simply:

"Even if everything I saw would have made me out to be evil, it would have been okay. Whatever this was that was with me, just loved me the way I was."[26]

After the review of my life I didn't want to return to my body.
I was comfortable there, and the light that surrounded me was pure love.
He [the Being of Light] asked me if I wanted to go back and I said no.
He then told me I had to go back, that there was more work to be done.
I was then sucked back into my body.
There was no other way to describe it.
Suddenly I was lying there, looking up at a doctor with paddles in his hand.

From *Transformed by the Light*

THE RETURN

THE RETURN to the body can happen at any number of stages along the near-death journey. Sometimes people are watching the resuscitation efforts of medical personnel from a dis-embodied perspective when, for example, shocks are applied with "paddles" to the chest to restart the heart and they simply find themselves "sucked back" into their bodies. One boy interviewed by Melvin Morse had suffered from nightmarish memories of this experience for years before he was finally able to speak about it. He had not been afraid of the rest of his expe-rience, he explained, but this violent jolt had terrified him.

One woman who had "died" in an automobile accident in which her small son Donnie was injured, hovered around long enough to make sure he was being looked after, and to telepathi-cally reassure him that he was going to be all right. Once she felt that everything was being taken care of, she began to explore her new disembodied existence and found its extraordinary freedom to be absolutely entrancing. Then, she says, "I heard my [deceased] grandmother speak my voice. I was sure it was her. She had that way of being teasing and serious at the same time. Grannie scolded me in a very loving way. 'Now you get back. You get back where you belong, Mousey!' Mousey had been her name for me when I was little. I didn't speak to her, but I was thinking to myself, 'No, I won't go back! It's so much nicer like this!' Grannie seemed to hear me anyhow and told me again to get back, that Donnie needed me and I still had a lot to do on earth.... To tell the truth, I still didn't really want to go back, but I knew it was my duty to."[27]

In fact, many of those who have been at the out-of-body stage of the experience but not entered the "tunnel" are those who seem to most commonly report a physical "jerk" or sensation

166

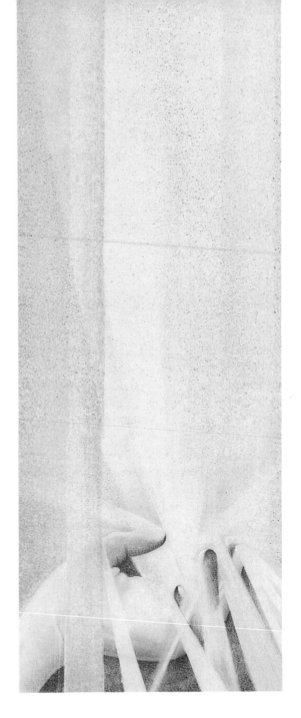

of being sucked back into the body – most notably as the result of shocks applied to the chest in resuscitation efforts, but also just as a result, say, of the body being touched by a member of a rescue team following an automobile accident. If they have not reached the stage of Donnie's mother, with her feeling of delight at the detachment from the weight of her physical existence, they may feel more relieved at having come back than anything else. But even this experience of knowing that they have a consciousness separate from their physical functioning can profoundly influence their lives and make them less fearful of death.

Michele Sorensen has become a near-death researcher herself, after nearly dying from complications of an injury as a teenager. In recalling her own experience, she tells of a telepathic conversation with a radiant white presence that she took to be a man.

"'You are dead, you know,' he said.

"'Yes, I know. It's great!'

"'Do you truly want to be dead?'

"'Oh, yes. Why not, this is all so wonderful!'

*Many travelers to the hereafter speak of being
shown beautiful, luminous landscapes
which sometimes feature "cities of light" and
centers of learning.*

Michele reports that she was able to continue observing the scene around her lifeless body below as she had this conversation, and was quite happy to let go of both family and friends. Even though she felt somewhat sad that they seemed so upset, she knew they would get over it, in time. Then the voice behind her prompted: "But look what you are missing." Then she was, she says, granted a vision of her future husband and family. She says, "I felt a longing for my husband and children even before I met them!" and she decided to return to her body.[28]

Generally, a feeling of reluctance to return is fairly common, but the strength of the reluctance seems to be related to the depth of the experience. The woman who wanted so badly to stay in the beautiful city of knowledge, for example, still feels some sorrow about her loss. Most of the reluctant return travelers tend to be those who have reached the stage where they have spent some time in the presence of the "being of light." Many of these people report that they returned not so much for their own benefit as for the benefit of others like children and family who needed them. Others might have felt a strong sense of something left undone that they wanted to accomplish, and still others have simply been "told" that it was not their time yet, and that they had "work to do" back on the earth. Nevertheless, some of them have been known to have a heated argument with the "gatekeeper" on being told they must go back.

One woman recounts her experience at the age of nine, when she nearly died from a high fever of undetermined origin. The doctors, as a last resort, had wrapped her in ice to bring her body temperature down, when she found herself wandering through a magical landscape of flowers and fields, including "the most gorgeous horses I had ever seen in the pasture off to the right." She was joined in her stroll by a luminous "presence" whom she describes as "friendly and not at all threatening" and who asked her where she was going. She explained that she wanted to go see the horses, and the presence accompanied her. "And I was talking to this blinding white light that was all colors and no colors at the same time. And it didn't have a face or features *per se*, but that didn't bother me. I remembered looking back down the tunnel at the people crowded around the bed and I didn't care that I was up here and my body was down there. I felt very good, as a matter of fact.

"So I was talking to this light and wandering over to these horses. I had just gotten my leg over the top rail of the fence and into the horse pasture when this voice out of nowhere said:

'What is she doing here?' And the light answered, 'She came to have the horses.' And the voice said: 'It's not right. It's not her time. She has to go back.'

"At this point I was clutching the rail because I didn't want to go back," she remembers. "That was the last thing I wanted to do. And the voice talked to the white light a little bit more and they decided that I would have to go back. So I threw a tantrum, I pitched a royal fit. I grabbed onto the rail of the fence and wrapped my arms and legs around it and I wouldn't let go. The voice just laughed. 'Look, you can have it later, but this is not the time. And throwing a tantrum is not going to do you any good.'"[29]

Sometimes, however rarely, the shoe is on the other foot. One woman reported that she was rather insistently being invited to stay, despite her own feelings of wanting to go back to the form of life she was more familiar with. "And I said, but I'm still young, I haven't danced enough yet! And he laughed, like a big belly laugh, and said okay, this time you can go back. But the next time, you have to stay."[30]

VARIATIONS ON THE THEME

NEAR-DEATH experiences have not happened to everybody who might have had the opportunity. Studies show that of those who have been "clinically dead" and brought back to life, perhaps less than half of them report one or more events similar to those which have been described. Why this is so, exactly, is still a mystery to be unraveled. The possible reasons are many, both medical and psychological, and all of them are being examined by dedicated researchers seeking clues to the mystery.

What is true, however, is that near-death experiences do happen to everybody in the sense that they have been reported by children and the elderly, the religious and the agnostic, the educated and the uneducated. They have even happened to infants, and as those infants have grown older their memories have remained with them. One woman didn't find out until she was twenty-nine years old that there was a phenomenon called the near-death experience, and that it shared much in common with a recurring dream she had had for most of her life. A chance conversation resulted in her being referred to Melvin Morse, and he tells her story in his book *Transformed by the Light*:

"This woman told me in detail about her recurring dream, one in which she finds herself floating out of her body and entering into a bright light. She said that the dream is vivid, and one that constantly reminds her of God. She also said that during the dream she has the sensation of being dead, although she has never really been sick in her life. In her dream she is drawn out of her body through a long, dark tunnel and enters into a beautiful and brightly lit place that makes her feel secure. While in this place she has a sense of understanding all of life, yet the precise nature of this understanding escapes her when she awakens."

The occurrence of a near-death experience is not
determined by factors like age, religious beliefs, or
the manner of death. Some people have even retained
memories of experiences they had as infants.

Morse listened sympathetically, but could not offer any immediate solution to the mystery of the source of her dream. Several months later, the woman herself returned with the answer: "One night, when she had the dream again, she asked the light why she could not get along with her father [with whom she had never had a good relationship]. A voice in the light spoke to her: 'Ask your mother about your birth.'

"A few days later she did just that, telling her mother of the dream and asking what happened during her birth. A torrent of guilt rushed from her mother. 'I had no idea that you could remember such a thing. I feel so guilty. I should have told you sooner. When I was eight months pregnant with you, I caught your father in an affair with his secretary. It was so traumatic for me that my placenta separated and you almost died during birth. The doctors really had to work to keep you alive.'"

Another of Morse's subjects, a boy named Mark, was only nine months old when he had a full cardiopulmonary arrest, and despite the fact that it took more than forty minutes for doctors to revive him he not only survived but thrived, with no evidence of any of the permanent damage that might be expected under such circumstances. His parents had never talked with him about his brush with death. But when he was three years old he was taken to a Christmas pageant, and afterwards he insisted that God didn't look like the man in the play at all. In response to his father's simple question about what he meant, Mark told the whole story. "I saw nurses and doctors standing over me trying to wake me up," he said. "I flew out of the room and saw Grandpa and Grandma crying and holding each other. I think they thought I was going to die." He had been in a long, dark tunnel and was trying to crawl up it to reach a bright light at the end, when a helping hand came along to support his journey. There was a "bright place" at the end, he said, where he "ran through the fields with God." He used the same language as the boy John had used, in his deathbed vision quoted previously. "You can double jump in heaven," Mark affirmed. God had asked him if he wanted to go back home, and Mark had said no. But he was sent back anyway, and told that he could return at another time.

According to Morse, Mark's memory of his experience remained quite vivid until he was five, when doctors removed a trachea tube they had inserted at the time of his near death. After that, the memory began to fade. "I suspect that the removal of the trachea signaled his subconscious

Not all near-death experiences are pleasant.
Instead of a welcoming light at the end of a tunnel,
a small minority of people report seeing the burning
flames of hell.

that he was no longer in danger of dying, and he began to lose memory. Now, Mark is a well-adjusted teenager who has high hopes of becoming a physical therapist or athletic trainer."

People who have attempted suicide have also had near-death experiences – and their journeys are often unpleasant, confirming the age-old taboo against taking one's own life. One exception to the rule, cited by Morse, is the story of the woman who wears the umbrella charm around her neck. Her abusive parents had made her life such hell by the time she was only seven years old that she decided to take her sled and aim headfirst into a concrete bench at the bottom of a hill. She succeeded in the effort, and recalls watching from outside her body as the children of her tough inner-city neighborhood took a cursory look at her wounds and went back to their play. She then floated upwards encased in her protective umbrella, until "suddenly I was in a very intense, bright light. I felt warm and loved in a way that I had never felt before. Then I heard a voice from the Light: 'You have made a mistake. Your life is not yours to take. You must go back.' I argued with the voice," she says, telling them "'No one cares about me.'" If she was hoping for sympathy, she didn't get it, at least in the ordinary sense of the word: "You're right," the voice answered. "No one on this planet cares about you, including your parents. It's your job to care for yourself."

It seems like a harsh message to deliver to a seven-year-old girl whose childhood was so horrific that she is still reluctant to speak of it today. But she came back to her body which, at this point, Morse points out "wasn't a pleasant place to be. She was in intense pain. Her mouth had been imbedded in a wooden railing around the bench. Her neck was broken. She tried to move her head and lost many of her teeth and a piece of her tongue." The girl decided at that point that as soon as she could, she would go back up the hill and try to kill herself again. Almost immediately she was once more engulfed by her "umbrella." This time she was treated to an awesome panorama of visions, including a magical view of a tree where she often played. The snow melt-

Some phenomena are similar to those
characteristic of pleasant experiences, but are
perceived to be dangerous or threatening.

ed from it and green leaves appeared, along with an image of herself sitting beneath the tree enjoying an apple. "I saw that the winter tree with the snow on it and the summer tree with the apples were two parts of a whole," she says now. "I saw that my life now was like the winter tree. And when I realized that the summer was ahead, I was willing to go back into my body." After she had spent many months in a coma, and then recovered enough to be sent home again, the girl was transformed. She began to stand up for herself, and, although she still suffers some paralysis from her injuries and jokes, "It wasn't as tough to get out of my body as it has been to get back in," she is now happily married with three children. The umbrella charm, she explains, helps her to remember that "when you hurt yourself, everything is hurt."[31]

People do have "bad trips" sometimes, however, whether or not their near-death experience is a byproduct of an attempt to commit suicide. Some researchers have suggested that these experiences actually take place while the person's body is still alive, and are more like dreams and nightmares than an actual near-death experience. In support of this theory, they point out that the patients' memories of negative experiences fade, while the memories of positive experiences remain clear and consistent, and even transform people's lives. Other researchers, more pessimistically inclined, say that of course the negative experiences tend to be repressed, and even suggest that perhaps others who have been near death but don't remember anything might have repressed the memory of a hellish journey.

But many of the reports of negative experiences bring to mind the old wisdom that one can be frightened almost to death by a rope lying in the middle of a dark road if one mistakes it for a snake. In this "mistaken identity" scenario, the glow of light at the end of a tunnel becomes the fire of hell, and the beckoning gestures of loving beings become a threatening array of demons

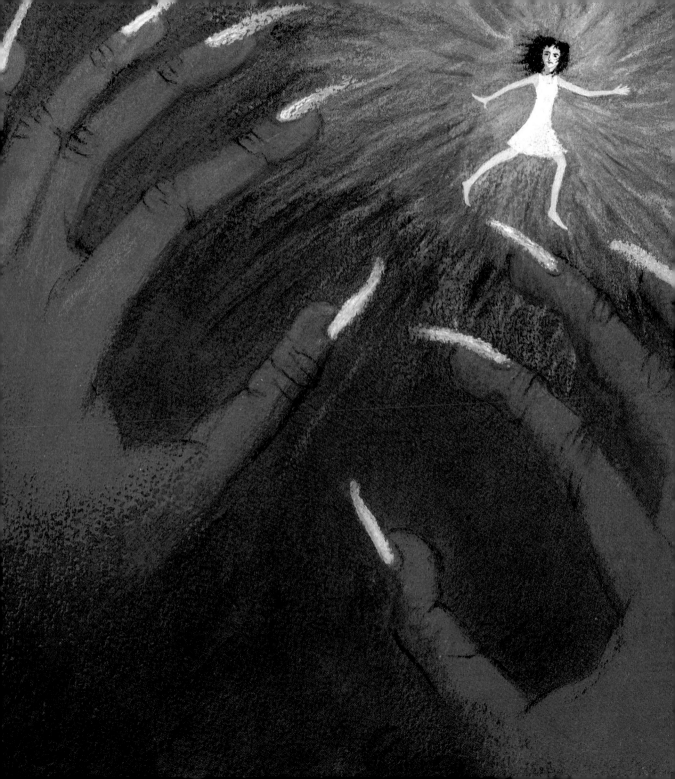

trying to drag one into the fire. A "being of light" might even become a lion. Take this story, for example:

"There was a big pit with vapor coming out and there were arms and hands coming out trying to grab mine... I was terrified that these hands were going to claw hold of me and pull me into the pit with them. As I lay there worrying what would happen next, an enormous lion bounded towards me from the other side and I let out a scream. I was not afraid of the lion, but I felt somehow he would unsettle me and push me into the dreadful pit. I remained in a state of semi-consciousness for about three days. I have never believed in hell, I feel God would never create such a place. But it was very hot down there, and the vapour or steam was very hot."[32] It is perhaps relevant to note that the woman telling the story had suffered from heat stroke.

Another common characteristic of negative experiences is that the sense of fear and panic, usually overcome quite early in the positive experiences, is never resolved. These people are apparently either unwilling or unable to "trust" or "let go" in the face of a situation that, perhaps just because of its sheer unfamiliarity, they find terrifying. As one woman, who found herself hovering over her body during a routine hysterectomy, says: "I felt very frightened and began to panic. I wondered why I was no longer in my body and thought I must be dead. I next found myself in a very frightening place, which I am sure was hell. I was looking down into a large pit, which was full of swirling gray mist and there were all these hands and arms reaching up and tying to grab hold of me and drag me in there. There was a terrible wailing noise, full of desperation. Then suddenly I found myself back in my body in the hospital bed."[33]

Of course, anyone who would like to believe that there is a "bad place" as well as a heavenly one waiting for us on the other side is free to do so, and many of us seem to believe that the threat of hell is needed to keep us in line. If such a place does exist, though – and if those who have undergone near-death experiences are representative of the population as a whole – then it seems that only about one in a hundred of us might end up going there. But there is no evidence to suggest that visits to hell are a result of particularly bad behavior or "sin." The most likely ticket to Dante's Inferno seems to be a combination of fear and panic – and in fact, even hellish journeys have been known to become pleasant ones for those who remain "dead" long enough to go more deeply into the experience.

Those things that the fathers perceived in a mirror and an enigma, but not in open revelation,
are now actually seen by some people, and are understood with greater certainty by others,
since they have heard them from those who have seen.
Many things previously unheard-of and hidden from mortal eyes, have been brought into the light;
things that once were doubted have become certain,
and things that lay completely concealed have been set out in clear view.
From *The Vision of the Monk of Eynsham,* 12th C., quoted in *Otherworld Journeys* by Carol Zaleski

The true value of existence is the connectedness that you have going with every other living thing....
Everything that happens to me now is a sense of awe.... What everyone talks about heaven being,
is right here and now. You just have to open up and see what's really going on.
Heading Towards Omega

PARADISE RECLAIMED

WHEN JAYNE SMITH had her near-death experience back in 1952, not very many people had ever heard of such a thing. After she had asked for, and received the answer to her question "What's it all about?" [page 158] she returned to her body. Once her condition had stabilized and she had regained consciousness, she recalls being wheeled back to her room still in "such a state of awe. As far as I knew, I was the only person in the entire world that this had ever happened to, because...I'd never heard of such a thing." She couldn't imagine what it meant, she says. "I knew it was the blessing of my life, but I didn't know what I was supposed to do with it."

Her first attempts to talk about it were not encouraging. She tried to tell her mother and father, who were present at her bedside when she first regained consciousness and could speak. "They didn't want to hear," she says. "I think I got out one and a half sentences and my father said, 'Put your head back, close your eyes. You've had a very bad time. Don't think about it.'"

"My husband, fortunately, didn't think that way at all," Jayne continues. "He knew that it was real." But it was perhaps harder for her husband to accept when Jayne would tell him how much she had wanted to stay in the presence of that wondrous light rather than coming back. "I would see this look of hurt cross his face. So finally, I stopped saying that because there's no way he could understand that there was nothing *personal* in this at all! And for weeks, I would have gone back any moment. And then, gradually, happily, that feeling leaves. You become

more a part of this world. For years I would have gone back almost any moment. Now I'm so entrenched here, I'm willing to wait my turn. I mean, I really like it, I'm having a good time!"[34]

More than forty years have passed since Jayne Smith's experience, and certainly more people, including medical professionals, know what Jayne didn't know at the time, that in fact such journeys happen to many when they are near death. But Western culture as a whole today still offers little in the way of understanding the deep transformation that can happen as a result of the near-death experience, or being able to support and learn from those who are transformed by it. That sense of being "in the world but not of it" expressed by so many who have returned from death is in fact the goal of all spiritual search and practice in the Eastern religions, and the goal of mystics everywhere. But it is decidedly not one with which most of us brought up in the Judeo-Christian West are familiar. Popular religion emphasizes "charity," or "involvement" or "good works" and "family values." The cool detachment from the world of a Gautam Buddha, or the "amoral" teachings of a Lao Tzu, are still somehow alien, despite a growing familiarity with these teachings among the young and educated in the Western world. The secular culture, on the other hand, emphasizes material success and accumulation – an interest which is clearly not valued at all in the luminous hereafter as glimpsed by those who have journeyed there.

In fact, the profound personal transformation undergone by many of those who have returned from death confronts us with a challenge to the very the meaning and substance of our lives. The transition they must make in rejoining our company, and the new vision required of those who wish to remain close to them after their return, can be shattering. Often, family members feel as if they quite literally have a "new person" to contend with.

Joe Geraci, when he died and came back, was a policeman with a family who had been brought up in the Roman Catholic Church. His own experience was so profound that he couldn't talk about it to anyone, including his wife, for six months or more. "It was such an emotional, beautiful, swelling feeling inside that every time I tried to express it, I think I would just explode, you know; I would break down and cry. And she, for the longest time couldn't figure out what was wrong with me."

*Those who have died and returned to life usually
find their former preoccupations have little meaning
and say that their primary concern is now to grow
in love and understanding.*

Joe can remember feeling angry, in fact, that he had been brought back to life – an anger which his wife had noticed, but which he could not find the words to explain. He describes the early period of his attempt to reenter the world as "probably the most frustrating six months of my existence." He had the feeling that he was starting life again, like a baby, and at the same time trying to somehow "hold on" to the perfection and peace that he had felt when he had been "dead."

"I began to bump into earthly things that you know, of course, aren't going to escape from you – they're there," he admits. One of the first collisions between his new self and his old world centered around the television: "There would be a commercial, a cosmetic commercial, I couldn't – I'd have to turn it off because it was something false, it was unnecessary, it was fake. It just didn't belong, [it was] insignificant. Any type of violence – if there was even an old Western, an old Western movie, I'd have to turn it off because to me that was total ignorance. There was just no reason on earth to show people killing people. That was frustrating, especially when the family was sitting down trying to watch television and Dad gets up and turns it off all the time! So I finally learned just to go to my room."

Finally, Joe found somebody he could really talk to, who seemed to understand. "I have a very, very close friend who is a priest, we call him Father Jim – who sat down with me a few times.... Here was a man I know did not experience what I did, but he seemed to know. He knew what I was talking about, very understanding. Perhaps the most important thing he did for me was to help me to readjust, to accept life, to understand that you are living, that, you know, that is there, it will come again. And that there is much more here, and that I was here for a reason."[35]

Having a "Father Jim," or someone like him on hand to listen and to understand becomes extraordinarily important for many people who find themselves almost like aliens on their return. Others find that they must leave situations which will not allow them to live in the new way demanded by their newly transformed selves. But whether their re-entry is difficult or easy, takes a matter of weeks or a matter of years, they are definitely transformed. It has even become, in the language of the researchers, one of the "characteristics" of the near-death experience itself.

It was a total immersion in light, brightness, warmth, peace, security.
I did not have an out-of-body experience.
I did not see my body or anyone about me.
I just immediately went into this beautiful bright light.
It's difficult to describe; as a matter of fact, it's impossible to describe.
Verbally, it cannot be expressed.
It's something which becomes you and you become it.
I could say "I was peace, I was love." I was the brightness, it was part of me....
You just know. You're all-knowing — and everything is a part of you.
It's — it's just so beautiful.
It was eternity.
It's like I was always there and I will always be there,
and that my existence on earth was just a brief instant.

Joe Geraci, Quoted in *Heading Toward Omega*

5

**FROM HERE
TO ETERNITY**

No longer in Lethean foliage caught
Begin the preparation for your death
And from the fortieth winter by that
    thought
Test every work of intellect or faith
And everything that your own hands have
    wrought,
And call those works extravagance of
    breath
That are not suited for such men as come
Proud, open eyed and laughing to the tomb.

W. B. Yeats, *Vacillation*

PREPARING FOR DEPARTURE

T HE MEDIEVAL stories of those who had been privileged to a glimpse of eternity provoked an interest in knowing how one might prepare for one's own journey when the time came. We have all but forgotten it now, but Western Christianity in the Middle Ages had its own version of the *Tibetan Book of the Dead*, in a collection of works known as the *Ars Moriendi*, or the "Art of Dying." In those days, death was a family affair at least, and in many cases involved the whole community. Hordes of people could be seen in the poorer quarters of the feudal cities following the priest on his rounds to administer last rites, and even squeezing themselves into whatever available space might remain around the bed of the dying. The aim of the "art of dying" literature became that of encouraging both the dying and those attending the deathbed to accept it as the "natural, necessary and universal" event it is clearly designed to be. "Death is nothing but a going [out] of prison, and an ending of exile," says the introduction to one such manual. "A discharging of an heavy burden, that is the body; finishing of all infirmities; a 'scaping of all perils; destroying of all evil things; breaking of all bonds; paying of the debt of natural duty; turning again into his country; and entering into bliss and joy."[1] Note the laudatory absence of threatening visions of hellfire!

In today's world, to "die with dignity" has become an altogether different sort of challenge than it was in the Middle Ages. The very words now conjure up visions of wires and tubes and

*India's Ganges is both a place of purification
for the living and sacred resting place for the
remains of the dead.*

dials and machinery capable of performing every act of "life" for the body except its brain function. Those who look on these visions of a sustained vegetative existence with horror have begun to make sure they have drawn up a "living will" or "advance directive" to specify what extraordinary measures may and may not be taken to prolong their lives if they are not in a position to voice their wishes directly. These documents may also list other desires, such as not being given more medication than is strictly necessary to deal with pain, or to be allowed to spend their last days in their own homes if at all possible.

In fact, the almost limitless capability of modern hospital technology to sustain life has directly contributed to the development of a "natural death" movement which parallels the "natural birth" movement of the past few decades. Most major cities in Europe and North America nowadays have some kind of organization to assist those who want to know about living wills, or those who want to make it possible for themselves or their loved ones to die at home rather than in a hospital. Slowly but surely, death is beginning to be spoken of in something above a whisper.

Far more controversial than efforts to avoid prolonging life by artificial means is the question of whether or not one ought to have the right to actively end one's life when that life seems to offer nothing more than unbearable physical suffering and pain. If we know we are going to die, and if we feel both psychologically and spiritually ready to drop a terminally ill and suffering body and enter into whatever awaits us beyond death, should we be able to hasten our own departure? Or, even more controversial, should we be able to terminate our own lives because we have a disease that we know will eventually leave us physically or mentally disabled?

In 1990 a Michigan doctor, Jack Kevorkian, brought these questions to the surface of public consciouness when he assisted the suicide of a woman in the early stages of Alzheimer's disease. The case was widely publicized, discussed, debated, and even sensationalized, with its eye-catching headlines about "Doctor Death" and his "Suicide Machine." But beneath the choppy waters of sensation lay much deeper questions to be explored – about what really constitutes a "life" that is worth the name, when and under what circumstances a person ought to be able to decide to end a life they no longer consider worth living, who ought to be allowed to help them, and how.

During the following year, in 1991, a more sober examination of these deeper questions was undertaken by author Derek Humphry. His book, *Final Exit*, openly discusses "the practicalities of self-deliverance and assisted suicide for the dying." To the astonishment of a previously wary publishing world, and the dismay of many physicians and religious leaders, the book headed straight for the New York Times bestseller list and stayed there for more than four months! Humphry as an individual, along with the Hemlock Society organization of which he is a part, makes a powerful argument that conscious human beings have the right to take charge of their own bodies, even to the point of embracing death when they feel the body has become too great a burden to bear. They continue to actively campaign for a law in North America, which they have titled the Death With Dignity Act, that would carefully define the circumstances under which it is permissible to assist another in ending his or her life. Anyone who gives such assistance now is liable to criminal prosecution.

But there is still a long way to go before it can be said that we are able to look death in the face with courage and love. Not only psychologically, but even in the most material and objective sense, it is still immensely difficult for many of us to accept. As anyone knows who has suddenly found themselves with the responsibility for dealing with the death of a family member, there are an enormous number of practical details to be taken care of during a time when one would much prefer to be free to cope with one's own emotions and feelings about the death. Funerals must be arranged, friends and relatives notified, certificates signed, and so on. Older people, who have generally had more experience in these matters, know this, and many of them want to spare their relatives as much of the bureaucratic agony as possible. But when they begin to speak about "making arrangements" for their own departure, they are too often scolded for being "morbid" and encouraged not to talk about such "nonsense."

It is time, as a society, that we recognize that preparing for death is not "nonsense" and that in fact, when the process of dying is undertaken consciously and with a spirit of adventure, it can be one of the greatest awakenings in life. The luminous visions shared by those who have returned from death have planted the seed of that recognition in our times. In order for that seed to grow, however, quite a few weeds must be cleared away from the ground where we have buried the whole subject of death for generations.

And Death is our sister, we praise Thee for Death,
Who releases the soul to the light of Thy gaze;
And dying we cry with the last of our breath
Our thanks and our praise.

The Song of St. Francis of Assisi

ANCIENT MAPS, MODERN GUIDES

ONE OF THE MOST important obstacles we face in accepting the death of the body as a natural and inevitable event, and nothing to be afraid of, lies in the fact that most of us think we *are* the body-and-mind complex, and that when it dies we will no longer exist. And indeed, if that is true, then why talk about it? "I'm alive now, right? And when I'm gone, I'm gone. Finished. Blotto. *Gone."* The problem is, our "remembrance" doesn't include this myth. Our remembrance includes myths of paradise, visions of hell, and any number of other scenarios, but it does not include the memory of utter and irrevocable extinction. So we don't believe it. We're caught in a terrible bind as a result. We've identified with the transient, which we can see from evidence all around us is going to die, and we have lost touch with the immortal, which nevertheless haunts us as a vague memory in our dreams. No wonder we would prefer not to talk about it. But talk about it we must, if we are to reclaim our immortality from the jaws of extinction and to wake up from the dream that we have lost our souls.

There are methods to recover our lost connection with that within us which never dies. Some of these methods are ancient, and some of them are new. Most of them, regardless of

*The effort of Eastern meditation practices is to
create a distance between the body and its
ego/personality and the witnessing spirit, or Self.*

their vintage, are called meditation, and their purpose is to create a perceptible space between the transient and the eternal, between the "Perceiver" and the events which it perceives, between the body and the soul.

A story is told about a man who came to the Sufi mystic Farid with a question: Why, he wanted to know, were the mystics so calm in the face of death? Farid did not answer him directly, but picked up a coconut from among those offered to him by his devotees, and asked the man to break it open, leaving the meat of the coconut intact. "Impossible!" said the man. "This coconut is not ripe, and the meat of it will adhere to the shell." Farid congratulated the man on his insight, and was about to dismiss him when the man protested that his question had not been answered. "I thought you must have got it," Farid said, "but you seem to be a little slow." He picked up a different coconut, handed it to the man, and repeated his request that he break it open, leaving the meat intact. This the man did, breaking the shell easily and handing Farid the kernel of coconut meat, intact. "Very good," Farid praised him. "Now you have the answer to your question." Seeing the puzzled look on the man's face, he continued. "The man who is afraid of death is like an unripe coconut – there is no distance between the outer shell and the essence, and he fears that when the shell is broken the essence will also fall to pieces. And he is right, as long as he remains unripe. If you want to be calm in the face of death, become ripe – create a distance between the outer shell and the inner man, so that when the shell is broken the essence will remain whole."[2]

What follows, then, is a sampling of methods to ripen the coconut.

DEVELOPING THE WITNESS

The first key to meeting even everyday hassles with some sort of equanimity is to be able to stand back from what is happening and watch it from the outside, as though it were some sort of movie rather than "real life." This ability to be an observer of one's own life, or to "witness" events without getting caught up in them is, as we have seen, good practice for the deathbed, and can turn a fearful situation into an exciting adventure. In fact, it's not a bad way to live, either. It can transform a Friday afternoon traffic jam into a chance to meditate, an insult into an

The key to Buddhist meditation techniques is to watch both one's own thoughts and external events without judging or becoming identified — just as if they were clouds passing across an empty sky.

opportunity to learn about the current state of one's self-esteem, or the end of a love affair into an occasion to celebrate one's newfound freedom. But this ability to watch the dramas of our own lives as though they were dramas on a stage is not one that most of us find natural. It is a knack that needs to be developed, and it requires practice. Most people find that it is easiest to begin with watching the activities of the body — walking, eating, taking a shower, whenever possible taking a distance and watching. Once this skill has been developed, then it is easier to be a witness to the more subtle activities of the mind and emotions.

Gautam Buddha's instruction for developing this witnessing capacity is this: Sitting silently, watch your breath coming and going. Simple, right? No, not so simple. Those who have tried it know that it can be one of the most difficult things in the world. First an itch arises, and must be scratched. A dog barks and you think about the dog you always wanted as a child, but your parents wouldn't let you have. This leads into a long and convoluted meander into the relationship you had with your parents, their relationship to each other, and your current efforts to avoid making their mistakes. Meantime your breath is coming and going automatically, without being watched at all. Or, if you are an earnest type, you are busy fighting with these thoughts, trying to suppress them, and they retaliate by coming faster and faster. Thus the second part of the instruction, which is to watch the thoughts in the same manner as you are watching the breath, letting them come and go, and bringing yourself back to watching the breath once they have gone. In the words of the contemporary meditation master Osho: "A few thoughts sometimes will come, let them pass — you just be indifferent, not concerned at all. If they come, good, if they don't come, good. Don't fight, don't push them away...if you don't want them, they will be very stubborn about going. You simply remain unconcerned, let them be there on the periphery as if traffic noise is there. And it is really a traffic noise, the brain traffic of millions of cells communicating with each other and energy moving and electricity jumping from one cell to another cell. It is just the humming of a great machine, so let it be there.... And you will be surprised — moments will come when the noise will disappear, completely disappear, and you will be left all alone."[3] The gap has been created, in other words; the coconut is becoming ripe. That witnessing consciousness which suddenly finds itself "left all alone" is able to see life as a play and, according to the mystics, that witnessing consciousness is what survives death.

THE TIBETAN BOOK OF THE DEAD

O child of noble family, when your body and mind separate, the dharmata will appear, pure and clear yet hard to discern, luminous and brilliant, with terrifying brightness, shimmering like a mirage on a plain in spring.
Do not be afraid of it, do not be bewildered.
This is the natural radiance of your own dharmata, therefore recognize it....

You have what is called a mental body of unconscious tendencies, you have no physical body of flesh and blood, so whatever sounds, colors and rays of light occur, they cannot hurt you and you cannot die. It is enough to recognize them as your projections. Know this to be the bardo state.

To the extent that the *Tibetan Book of the Dead* is incomprehensible, it is because Western civilization has only a passing acquaintance with the notion that the real "self" consists of a witnessing consciousness. As Francesca Fremantle points out in the foreword to one translation of this ancient text on the art of dying, this presents a difficulty even in the language used in translation: "Western thought has developed along very different lines from that of the East, and so if an English word is chosen from the vocabulary of philosophy or religion, it will inevitably contain all kinds of associations and implications which may be quite alien to the underlying assumptions of Buddhism."[4] In fact, as Fremantle points out, a more compatible language can be found in contemporary Western psychology, which has by and large abandoned ideas like "sin" and "evil" in favor of morally neutral terms like "neurosis." It also uses words like "projection" to

The Tibetan Book of the Dead *is designed to be
read in the presence of the corpse and describes
various "peaceful and wrathful deities" to be
encountered on the journey to the beyond.*

describe the phenomena of seeing the outside world not as it really is, but through the colored glasses of our own ideas, expectations, and beliefs.

The Tibetan Book of the Dead was translated into English in the early part of this century. All its instructions are designed, in accordance with Buddhist teachings, to help the dying person to become free from earthly attachments and desires and thereby move towards liberation, or the "perfect buddha state" where there is no return to physical life in another body. The book is set out in a series of steps, each apparently based on a knowledge of what we are likely to experience in the moments just before death, and in the days following it. With this understanding, the text is designed to be read aloud in the presence of the corpse or, if the corpse has already been cremated or otherwise disposed of, with the attention of the reader directed to the dead person's wandering spirit. At each stage of the journey into death, then, the spirit of the dead person is given an opportunity to become one with the "luminosity" that he or she will find along the way.

Since these texts are based on specific Tibetan teachings, these luminosities are given various colors, names, and functions corresponding to the teachings. But there are striking parallels to be found within these ancient Tibetan texts to modern accounts of the near-death experience – perhaps most notably, the reports of two different sorts of "light beings." In modern accounts, one kind of "light being" is perceived as either escort or greeter to the other world, most often a deceased relative or friend. The second is the overwhelmingly loving "Being of Light" who assists in the life review. In the Tibetan system, this latter Being of Light is the "pure luminosity of the dharmata" and merger with it assures enlightenment and ultimate liberation. The former kind of light beings are the projections of the dying person's own mind, and to be avoided because they will lead him or her ultimately back into another rebirth.

The Tibetans are very generous in giving the dead many opportunities to achieve liberation. The process of reading from the *Book of the Dead* can go on for as long as seven weeks, which is felt to be the longest time a departed spirit might wander in the "bardo" or the gap between death and the next life, before taking another physical body. If all efforts toward leading the person towards liberation fail, then the soul is guided in choosing a suitable womb so that he or she will be born in the best possible circumstances to continue developing towards liberation in the life to come.

O child of noble family, listen.
Now the pure luminosity of the dharmata
is shining before you; recognize it.
O child of noble family,
at this moment your state of mind is by
nature pure emptiness,
it does not possess any nature whatever,
neither substance nor quality such as
color, but it is pure emptiness;
this is the dharmata, the female
buddha Samantabhadri.
But this state of mind is not just
blank emptiness, it is
unobstructed, sparkling, pure and
vibrant; this mind is the male
buddha Smanatabhadra.
These two, your mind whose
nature is emptiness without
any substance whatever, and
your mind which is vibrant and
luminous, are inseparable:
this is the dharmakaya
of the buddha.
This mind of yours is
inseparable luminosity and
emptiness in the form of a
great mass of light, it has no
birth or death, therefore it is
the buddha of Immortal Light.
To recognize this
is all that is necessary.
When you recognize this pure
nature of your mind as
the buddha, looking into your
own mind is resting in the
buddha-mind.

MEDITATING ON DEATH – THE TANTRIC WAY

*Focus on fire rising through your form from the toes up
until the body burns to ashes but not you.*

Vigyan Bhairav Tantra

Gautam Buddha used to send his disciples to India's cremation grounds to meditate on the impermanence of the physical body. In the West, the process of cremation usually takes place out of sight in high-tech, non-polluting chambers specially built for the purpose. But in India, for example, burnings are held today in much the same way as they have been held for centuries. The body is bathed, dressed, bound to a stretcher and covered with flowers before being carried to a special site, often near a river, to be burned. There, it is laid on a pyre constructed of as much sandalwood as the family can afford, mixed with other wood and stacked neatly around the body. Gaps are left in this construction so that the face of the deceased is visible, and a staff can later be inserted to smash the skull open so the soul can be finally freed from the burning body.

This whole process can bring the observers face-to-face with the end of the physical body in a way that none of our Western ceremonies do – and it is also seen as a help to the spirits of the dead to recognize their condition and to accept that they are no longer part of the physical world.

The tantric method of visualizing one's own death will be much easier for those who have actually been able to witness an outdoor cremation of the type held in India or other parts of Asia. If this is not possible, some alternative suggestions to help the visualization are offered in commentaries by Osho on the *Vigyan Bhairav Tantra* where the meditation is given.[5] He recommends "warming up" for the visualization by practicing a breathing technique which focuses on exhalation. Otherwise, he says, our usual fear of death will prevent us from allowing the visualization to go very deep. "A readiness is needed," he says, "otherwise the technique will not be of much help. And you can be ready only if you have tasted death in a certain way." His recommendations are as follows:

Tantra believes in encountering one's deepest fears
directly, and provides a number of meditation
techniques to prepare for death which involve a
kind of "rehearsal" for what is to come.

"If you want to enter this technique you must be aware of this deep fear [of death.] And this deep far must be thrown away, purged, only then can you enter the technique. This will help: pay more attention to exhalation...forget inhaling. Don't be afraid that you will die; you will not die – the body will inhale by itself. You need not interfere. Then a very deep relaxation will spread all over your conciousness. The whole day you will feel relaxed, and an inner silence will be created.

"You can deepen this feeling more if you do another experiment. Just for fifteen minutes in the day exhale deeply. Sit in a chair or on the ground, exhale deeply, and while exhaling close the eyes. When the air goes out, you go in. And then allow the body to inhale, and when the air goes in, open the eyes and you go out. It is just the opposite: when the air goes out, you go in; when the air goes in, you go out.

"When you exhale, space is created within, because breath is life. When you exhale deeply, you are vacant, life has gone out. In a way you are dead, for a moment you are dead. In that silence of death, enter within. Air is moving out: you close your eyes and move within. The space is there and you can move easily.

"Remember, when you are inhaling to move inwards is very difficult, because there is no space to move. While exhaling you can move within. And when the air goes in, you go out; open the eyes and move out. Create a rhythm between these two. Within fifteen minutes you will feel so deeply relaxed, and you will be ready to do this technique....

Focus on fire rising through your form from the toes up....

"Just lie down. First conceive of yourself as dead; the body is just like a corpse. Lie down, and then bring your attention to the toes. With closed eyes move inwards. Bring your attention to the toes and feel that the fire is rising from there upwards, everything is being burned. As the fire rises, your body is disappearing. Start from the toes and move upwards.

"Why start from the toes? It will be easier, because the toes are very far away from your 'I', from your ego. Your ego exists in the head. You cannot start from the head, it will be very difficult, so start from the farthest-away point...the toes. Feel that the toes are burned, only ashes remain, and then move slowly, burning everything that the fire comes across.... The fire is rising upwards and the parts it has passed are no more, they have become ashes. Go on upwards, and lastly the head disappears. Everything has become ashes...the dust has fallen into dust....

...until the body burns to ashes but not you.
"You will remain just a watcher on the hill. The body will be there – dead, burned, ashes – and you will be the watcher, you will be the witness."

Osho, *Vigyan Bhairav Tantra*

OUT-OF-BODY PRACTICE RUNS

The contemplative path of some of the meditations described in the previous section may not appeal to some. And the *Tibetan Book of the Dead* might seem either too obscure, or too ritualistic to suit others. In that case, the "magic carpet ride" of an out-of-body experience will achieve the same effect and, if learned properly, can provide hours of entertainment while you await the time scheduled for you to experience the real thing. "Astral projection" manuals abound in today's high-tech culture, but the technology itself is as ancient as the monasteries of Tibet. No special tools are needed for the adventure either, other than a healthy quotient of daring, a comfortable place to lie down, some ability to visualize, and, in one exercise given below, the help of a couple of good friends who won't think you're crazy to be trying to achieve this "impossible" thing. Keep in mind, though, that people have sometimes been terrified by the experience when it has happened to them unexpectedly. You might want to read more about it before actually experimenting yourself, and a few titles are recommended in the further reading list at the back of the book.

AN OVERVIEW

According to theories of the Theosophists – derived from various Eastern teachings, and the Tibetan tradition particularly – each of us has several "bodies" in addition to the physical. The etheric body, or "double," is an extension of the physical body whose function is to keep the physical body in contact with the other, higher bodies. At death, this body leaves and finally dissipates; otherwise it rarely separates from its physical counterpart.

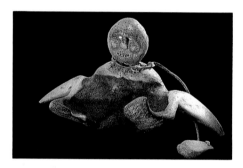

Beyond the etheric body is the astral body which is said to be the center of the senses and desires. The astral body can separate from the physical body and, because it carries with it both consciousness and sense perception, is able to observe the physical body from outside, to see, hear and understand everything that is happening in its surroundings. It can travel great distances in the astral world, either in sleep or consciously, at will. This is what is referred to as astral projection.

The astral body is believed to be connected to the physical body by a cord, silver in color, and it is through this cord that the person is able to return to the physical body. The cord is a kind of lifeline; when the cord is cut there is no possibility of return, and the person dies. This idea seems to underlie the belief in many tribal cultures where shamanism is practiced, that it is important not to wake a sleeping shaman suddenly, or to interfere when he or she is in an entranced state. They don't use the language of astral travel, but shamans are known to journey into the spirit worlds, and these journeys are probably the same as "astral" travels. At death, the breaking of the cord allows the higher bodies to leave, taking the essence or "spirit" to higher worlds. Similar imagery is also found in the beliefs of many tribal peoples.

Sylvan Muldoon is perhaps one of the best-known astral travelers.[6] An American who says that he has been able to travel astrally from childhood, he describes the experience as beginning with the inability to move, called "astral catalepsy." This is followed by a floating sensation, accompanied by a feeling of vibration and pressure in the back of the head. The floating "body" is horizontal at first and shifts to a vertical position when the ability to move returns. Muldoon

has observed that the silver cord joins the two bodies from the back of the head of the astral body to a spot between the eyes of the body below. The cord changes in thickness, he says, becoming thinner as the astral body moves further away from its physical counterpart. Others report that the cord joins the two bodies at the navel.

Muldoon says that projection can occur temporarily as the result of a shock or blow, or even sitting in a car that has stopped short. He also speculates that such sensations as the bodily jerk sometimes experienced before falling asleep can be an indication of a projection about to take place, but suddenly interrupted by waking consciousness. Parapsychological research has been conducted in which it seems that certain people are indeed capable of "astral travel," though the more elaborate features of the Theosophical model such as the silver cord, and the existence of several "higher bodies," have not been confirmed. For those who want to try it, the following suggestions have been offered by experienced travelers.

IMAGINING NO-BODY-NESS

Many people report that simply imagining that it is possible to float upwards out of their bodies allows them to do so. The following suggestions are adapted from their experiments.

1. Lie on your back in a comfortable position, having removed all jewelry and tight clothing, and making sure you will not be disturbed. Relax both body and mind, breathing deeply and rhythmically with your mouth partly open, until you feel that you are drifting towards sleep. Now imagine that you are floating up off the bed, and retain this image until you are able to feel that you are no longer touching the bed. Then experiment with moving higher, floating above the body but still in a horizontal position. When you feel ready, slowly assume a vertical position and travel away from your body.

2. Imagine a duplicate of yourself hovering above you with its back towards you. Imagine it in as much detail as possible, the hair, the kind of clothing it is wearing, and so on. As your duplicate begins to become more real, your own physical position may start to feel uncertain, and there may be a period of confusion. Keep your attention focused on the back of the imagined double, and when the double has become stable, shift your consciousness out of your watching body and into the floating one.

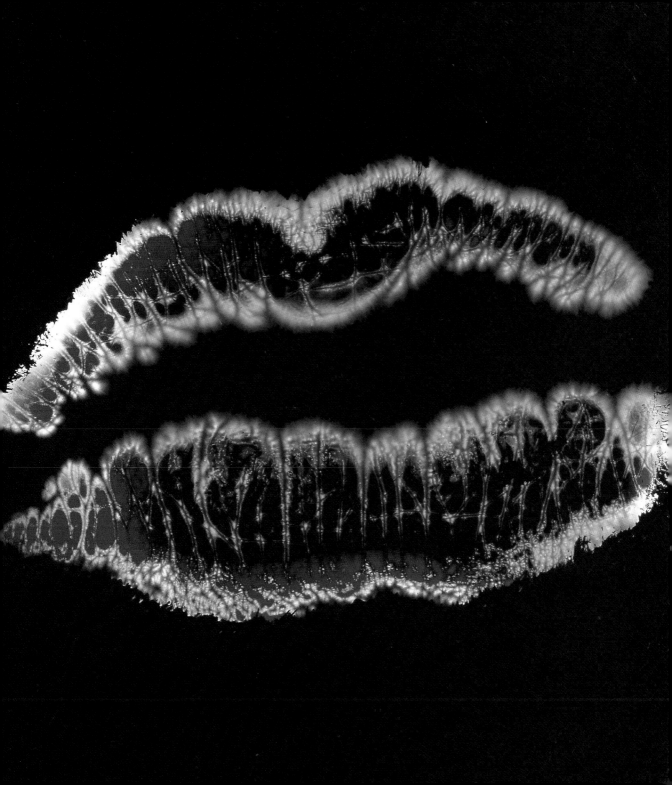

Experienced astral travelers report that there seem to be several different "realities" available to us when we are out of the body that can be quite different from the everyday reality we normally perceive.

OBE CARTOGRAPHY

Men seem to find the following method easier, for some reason – especially those who are not very adept at visualization.

Pick a route you are very familiar with, such as the path between two rooms in your house, and choose six different "landmarks" of the journey. Before starting the experiment, spend two or three minutes looking at each of these six points and planting them firmly in your mind. Lie down in a comfortable position, spend a few minutes relaxing, slowing your breathing and allowing your mind to still itself. Now imagine that you are in a position to see the first point, just as you were before you lay down. Move in this way from one point to another, until you have made the whole journey. If you practice this method before going to sleep, after a few nights your imagination can be strengthened to the point where you feel that your normal consciousness and sense perceptions are actually making this journey.

TRAVELING COMPANIONS

This technique is done with the help of two other people. In a warm, darkened room, the traveler lies down while one helper massages the feet and the other vigorously massages the head. A tingling and buzzing sensation should result, with the body of the traveler feeling light, or as if it is changing shape. One of the helpers then asks the traveler to imagine his or her feet stretching out by one or two inches, and then the head. Alternate suggestions of extending the feet and the head are given, so that the traveler's body length is gradually increased by about one or two feet. Then the suggestion is given that both ends of the body expand outwards at the same time, finally filling up the whole room like a balloon.

One of the helpers should then guide the subject in traveling to a spot outside the front door, and ask that he or she describe all the details of the surroundings there. Then the traveler is guided to rise up into the sky above the house until the surrounding countryside or city can be seen. Being asked to describe each stage of the journey, and to change the scene at will – say, from day to night, or to turn the lights on and off – will reassure the subject that the scene is under his or her control, and thereby avoid feelings of fear or panic. Then the traveler can be invited to fly off and land wherever he or she wishes to go.

TAKE IT EASY

The following instructions offered by Osho require a knack for focused attention, but aside from that are perhaps the simplest of all:

"Simply using your total willpower you can draw your consciousness inside from all parts of your body. You close your eyes and feel that the consciousness is shrinking inward. You feel the energy moving away from your hands and feet towards the inside. You see the energy moving down from your head. The energy begins to converge upon the center from where it originated — the rays begin to withdraw from all points. If this experiment is carried on with an intense feeling, in an instant the whole body becomes dead; only one point remains inside alive. The entire body becomes lifeless, while the inner core remains alive like a flame. This living center can now be experienced very well as something separate from the body.... Then just think of going out of the body, and you will be out of your body.... Just a desire to come out of the body, and the phenomenon occurs. And again, just a desire to get back into the body, and it is back in."[7]

Man imagines that it is death he fears;
but what he fears is the unforeseen, the explosion.
What man fears is himself, not death.

Saint-Exupery, *Flight to Arras* (1942) tr. Lewis Galantiere

Death's stamp gives value to the coin of life;
making it possible to buy with life
what is truly precious.

Rabindranath Tagore, *Stray Birds*

WHAT TO UNPACK

I F LIFE AND DEATH are in fact just two sides of one coin – if the sages are right in saying that it is by living well that we learn to die well – then it follows that the most important preparation for *dying* with a sense of adventure and acceptance is to *live* with a sense of adventure and acceptance. Superficially, this seems to be a contradiction: if we are enjoying life to the fullest, then surely we will be all the more reluctant to die. But our experience tells us this is not the case. Viewed from the outside, for example, death seems more tragic when it strikes children or young people in their prime than it does when it befalls those who have had their chance to live out their allotted "threescore and ten." We can even accept the deaths of younger people when it is clear that they have succeeded in making their mark on the world, when we have a sense that they have been able to accomplish what they were meant to do here among us. Even though we might be saddened by their passing, we are comforted by our shared understanding that at least these people have siezed the opportunity to live well. Our innate wisdom about the harmony of life and death surfaces despite the apparent contradictions, and tells us that these departures are not only somehow "okay" but also instructive – we are reminded, if only for a moment, that life offers no guarantee of tomorrows, and if we are not to be filled with regrets when our own time comes we must do the important things today. And this sense of urgency arises not only in light of our own ultimate departure, but also the departure of those we care for, lest our grieving be multiplied by the fact that our love has remained unexpressed, or our transgressions unacknowledged and unforgiven.

Really, to the extent that we understand the naturalness, inevitability and universality of death, our attitudes toward life itself are profoundly affected. We cannot travel lightly and joyously through life, nor can we enter death with a spirit of adventure, if we are laden with suitcases full of regrets about the past and postponements for the future. In this sense, the suffering of those who know they are going to die is compensated – they at least have time to unpack their suitcases, to settle their accounts in preparation for their departure. But in a society which has made death one of its greatest taboos, we often try to deny even this opportunity to the dying, and conspire with doctors to withhold the truth from the terminally ill. In doing so we risk achieving the opposite of what we intend. Our hope is to make the passage somehow easier, while in fact we may be only contributing to its ultimate difficulty and sorrow.

The messages brought back by those who have been privileged have a firsthand vision of the hereafter are many, and profound. At the heart of them all, however, lies the opportunity to begin to see life and death as a seamless whole, to be allowed a godlike glimpse of both sides of the coin, simultaneously. Furthermore, they confirm our deepest understandings of the truth – that love and understanding, not power and material possessions, are what counts in the end. This reminder challenges us to settle our own accounts, individually, to unpack our own suitcases by whatever means are available to us. Sometimes it can be as simple as a phone call, a letter, or a heartfelt conversation. Often it can be difficult – many of us carry a heavy load of past frustrations and regrets, and many others are burdened with an everyday load of duties and responsibilities that bring them little joy. We generally seem to have neither the time nor the encouragement to stop long enough to take a look at the baggage we are carrying and decide whether it is sustaining and nourishing our lives or, on the contrary, dragging us down. And opening up the suitcase of past regrets can even be painful, especially if they have been repressed rather

> *In accepting the inevitability of death, and in being*
> *willing to prepare for it consciously, we increase*
> *our chances of undertaking the journey with*
> *equanimity and a spirit of adventure.*

than acknowledged. Every mystic tradition tells us that we must face our demons before we are privileged to stand in the light, whether that process take the form of the cleansing fires of purgatory or the healing waters of baptism. If we are to be resurrected into a "here" which leads seamlessly into a "hereafter" we must allow our old selves to die first.

"Our last garment is made without pockets," says the Italian proverb...a more poetic version of the English-language truth that "you can't take it with you." The journey of death demands that we unpack, and divest ourselves of all that fills our pockets and prevents the heart from being lighter than a feather. It is true not only of past accumulations, but of all the "to-do's" on our list that we have left undone. The *Handbook of Natural Death*, published by the Natural Death Centre in London, contains one exercise that will be particularly helpful for those who want to assess their luggage in preparation for their departure. It goes as follows:

Imagine that you know you are to die within days and complete as many of the following sentences as you find suitably provocative:

Outside observers would probably say that my main achievements have been...

For myself, what I am most pleased with and proud of in my life are...

One of the most important lessons that I have learned in my lifetime is that...

During my life I have used my...[list three positive personal characteristics, for example: imagination, sense of humor and intelligence] through my...[list three activities, for example: writing, running groups and parenting] with the underlying vision, I now realize, of helping work towards a world in which, one day...[describe your long-term Utopia, for example: "people are kind and sensitive to each other, nature is at ease and magic is alive"].

The people I have felt closest to in my life have been...

One generalization I could make about the quality of my relationships with others is that...

If I regret anything, it is that...

If I had known how short a time I had left to live, I would probably have...

The editors of the handbook point out that the purpose of the exercise, besides that of evaluating your achievements and failures, is to discover whether a more acute awareness of your own mortality would lead you to want to make changes in your life, in case you might wish to make them now rather than being filled with regrets on your deathbed.

As Zen Master Taji approached death, his disciples assembled at his bedside.
One of them, remembering that the master was especially fond of a certain kind of cake, had spent
half the day searching the pastry shops of the town for this confection, which was now presented to
the Master. With a wan smile the dying man accepted the cake, and began slowly to eat it. As he
grew weaker and weaker, one of the disciples inquired whether he had any final words for them.
"Yes," the master replied.
Anxious not to miss a single word, all the disciples leaned forward to hear what he had to say.
"This cake is delicious!" said Taji, and then slipped away.

THE FLIGHT OF THE ALONE
TO THE ALONE

IN THE EAST, "the flight of the alone to the Alone" is used to describe both the phenomenon of enlightenment, the death of the ego with its illusion of separateness from the rest of the universe, and the death of the physical body, with its release of the spirit so it can return to the source which is its eternal home. The emphasis on the word "alone" is intentional. We are alone here in our life on earth, say the mystics of the East, despite our connections with others

through work and family. We may try to avoid seeing the evidence of that aloneness as it shows itself in countless ways, but we cannot avoid the truth of it. And nowhere is the truth so clear as when we are facing death, and see that we must ultimately face it alone. We are Alone with a capital A, they say, when we finally depart for good, never to return. The Tibetan Buddhists, for one, would agree with the letter, if not the spirit, of scientific assertions that the luminous beings and family members who have greeted those near death are just "projections" of the mind. The views of scientists and Eastern mystics would diverge at this point, however, with the mystics asserting that these projections are fully as "real" as the familiar, everyday reality. Furthermore, these "projections" will guide the spirit back into taking a new form in the everyday reality if the spirit is not quite ready to face the terror and the glory of being ultimately Alone – dissolved into the oneness where neither "I" exists, nor "thou" to comfort the "I" in the eternity of its loss.

For most of us, that ultimate journey to the Alone is utterly incomprehensible, and its terrors far outweigh any abstract idea of the glory that the actual experience – or, rather, absence of experience as we know it – might contain. Even to contemplate it can bring us full

circle to the primal terror of extinction we faced back in the days when we saw our families and friends getting ripped apart by wild animals. That is no doubt the reason the Tibetans developed such an elaborate and insistent set of guidelines to reassure the dead on their journeys, and why most other forms of Buddhism, with the notable exception of Zen, developed layers of heavens and hells like so many other religions, to give concrete and familiar form to the abstract and unknowable formlessness that awaits us in the hereafter. Zen, on the other hand, with its down-to-earth emphasis on the herenow, insists that we go on unpacking our suitcases every moment so as to be ready for any journey, whatever form it takes. In their emphasis on trust rather than belief, the Zen people assure us that whatever route the road might take, it will always lead us "here" and we will be walking through "here" every step along the way. This is the message of Zen Master Taji to his disciples, eager as they were to hear some great revelatory truth: In this moment, "This cake is delicious." The next moment will take care of itself.

Meantime, most of us have much to learn, and perhaps even more to unlearn, before we can face not only death but life itself with the equanimity of a Master Taji. It is almost irrelevant which side of the coin we choose to polish first. This book has focused on bringing death back from its remote and hidden shadows, and into the sacred and central place in life where it belongs. It could have as easily focused on bringing back life – as distinct from a competitive race to accumulate more than we know how to use intelligently – into harmony with the sacred natural rhythms of a universe that we all seem to remember as paradise. Because, as we can easily see when we take the time and distance to look, each "here" has flowered (or decayed, as the case may be) from a previous "here" and each "now" flows naturally into the "now" of the moment to come. In a sense, we must "die" each moment – whether we like it or not – to make a space for the new moment to come. And unless we allow this constant renewal we run the risk of being more dead than alive even while we are still breathing. Both the *Tibetan Book of the Dead* and the medieval *Ars Moriendi* stress the importance of learning to die not only at the end of life, but as a means of enhancing the life we are living here and now. "Against his will he dieth that hath not learned to die," warns one *Ars Moriendi* text. "Learn to die and thou shalt learn to live, for there shall none learn to live that hath not learned to die."

Death may, in the end, be just a mirror,
reflecting the attitudes and feelings
we are carrying when we approach its door.

The "hereafter" will greet all of us, whether it comes by surprise or after a period of anticipation, with a mirror. Whether that mirror reflects the luminous glory of the heaven within us or unleashes the repressed demons of a lifetime depends, I suspect, very much on what we are carrying with us when we pass through the door.

To get ready for the passage we have work to do both individually and as a society, right here on earth. Jayne Smith is one who returned from death and speaks eloquently of the world she found herself seeing through new eyes: "When you've experienced total, unconditional love, and then you are back in this world and can't find it anywhere, it leaves a kind of empty feeling," she says. And in her case, the unconditional love was not even to be found in the place our society has always said it should be, either. "After my near-death experience I couldn't wait to go back to church. So I went...and heard a sermon on smoking and drinking. I found it a terrible letdown. I went other times, but the sermons weren't on anything that matters.... I know God is about joy and I kept waiting for some minister to tap into love and joy and celebration, and to tell his congregation 'you are love.' Because that's what we are."[8]

"I believe love can be just as infectious as hate," says Joe Geraci. "It has to turn around. And to do that, people have to start somewhere. On a small scale, just me telling you about my experience, and someone reading what you're going to write. It multiplies quickly. And I'm not the only one who has had this experience. There are thousands of us all around the world. Multiply my story by a thousand and you'll see how quickly it can grow. It can be done. In fact it has already started."[9]

Words like these, coming from people in our own time, have a ring of authenticity that the passage of years and gathering of dust has obscured in so many of our ancient religious scriptures. The visions of the hereafter which have been brought back by those who have made the journey "from death to deathless life" as the *Upanishads* say, echo to the essential truths of all our scriptures, and challenge us to once again bring those truths back to the center of our lives. In doing so, we have the opportunity to "grow up" in a way, to put behind us once and for all the fears and superstitions of our ancestors and, in embracing both sides of the coin of life and death, find ourselves infinitely richer than we have ever been before.

To civilize death, to bring it home and make it no longer a source of dread, is one of the great challenges of the age.... Gradually, dying may come to hold again the place it used to occupy in the midst of life: not a terror but a mystery so deep that man would no more wish to cheat himself of it than to cheat himself of life.

The Natural Death Handbook

FAMOUS LAST WORDS

"In spite of myself I go on hoping.... I hope with all my heart there will be painting in heaven."
Jean Corot

"I am not the least afraid to die."
Charles Darwin

"I must go in; the fog is rising."
Emily Dickinson

"It is very beautiful over there."
Thomas A. Edison (momentarily emerging from a coma)

"Mozart!"
Gustav Mahler

"More light!"
Johann Wolfgang von Goethe

"I suffer much less. The music is so beautiful... Listen, listen in the midst of all those voices I recognize my mother's!"
Louis XVII

"Does nobody understand?"
James Joyce

"Mamasha!" (Mother!)
Waslaw Nijinsky

"Crito, we owe a cock to Aesculapius. Don't neglect this."
Socrates

"Get my 'Swan' costume ready.
Anna Pavlova

"It is all light."
George Augustus Selwyn (Bishop of Lichfield)

"Sister, you're trying to keep me alive as an old curiosity, but I'm done, I'm finished, I'm going to die."
George Bernard Shaw (to his nurse)

"Now I want to go home."
Vincent VanGogh

"I still live... Pretty..."
Daniel Webster

"This is the last of earth! I am content."
John Quincy Adams

"Beautiful."
Elizabeth Barrett Browning

"Pure and amiable spirit...pure and amiable spirit...pure and amiable spirit."
Antonio Canova, sculptor

"Take away these pillows—I shall need them no more."
Lewis Carroll

"Don't be afraid."
Charles XII of Sweden

"Now I am at the source of blessedness."
Frederic Chopin

"My lord, the crown which I have borne so long has given enough of vanity in my time. I beseech you not to augment it in this hour when I am so near my death."
Queen Elizabeth I
(to the Archbishop of Canterbury)

"I am resting. This rest is magnificent; more beautiful than words can tell."
John Ericsson

"I've never felt better."
Douglas Fairbanks

"I am making my last effort to return that which is divine in me to that which is divine in the universe."
Plotinus

"I do not feel anything but a certain difficulty of existing."
Bernard de Fontenelle

"Why do you weep? Did you think I was immortal?"
Louis XIV

"See the sun, whose smiling face calls me; see that immeasurable light. There is God! Yes, God Himself, who is opening His arms and inviting me to taste at last that eternal and unchanging joy that I had so long desired."
Jean Jacques Rousseau

"God bless you all; I feel myself again."
Sir Walter Scott

When his hour for death had come,
He slowly rais'd himself from the bed on the floor,
Drew on his war-dress, shirt, leggings, and girdled the belt around his waist,
Call'd for vermillion paint (his looking-glass was held before him),
Painted half his face and neck, his wrists, and back-hands,
Put the scalp-knife carefully in his belt—then lying down, resting a moment,
Rose again, half sitting, smiled, gave in silence his extended hand to each and all,
Sank faintly low to the floor (tightly grasping the tomahawk handle),
Fix'd his look on wife and children—the last.

From "Leaves of Grass" by Walt Whitman (describing the death of Osceola,
a Seminole who "literally died of a broken heart" in prison at Fort Moultrie in Florida)

"A little whille and I will be gone from among you, whither I cannot tell. From nowhere we come, into nowhere we go. What is life? It is the flash of a firefly in the night. It is a breath of a buffalo in the winter time. It is as the little shadow that runs across the grass and loses itself in the sunset."

Crowfoot, Chief of the Blackfoot Confederacy

219

NOTES

INTRODUCTION

1 Blaise Pascal. *Pensées* (1670); trans. W.F. Trotter.

2 *Otherworld Journeys* by Carol Zaleski is a thought-provoking and thoroughly readable examination of the differences and similarities between medieval and contemporary near-death experiences and their cultural and spiritual significance.

3 The story of the tennis shoe was reported by Kimberly Clark in the anthology, *The Near-Death Experience – Problems, Prospects, Perspectives.* Dr. Sabom's book also contains many well-documented reports from resuscitated patients who witnessed in detail the events happening around them when they were "dead." (See Bibliography.)

CHAPTER I

1 Ovid, *Metamorphoses.* Translated in *Primitivism and Related Ideas in Antiquity,* by Arthur Lovejoy and George Boas. Baltimore: Johns Hopkins Press, 1935.

2 *Chuang Tzu.* Burton Watson, trans. New York: Columbia University Press, 1964.

3 Extracted from the poem, "Intimations of Immortality from Recollections of Early Childhood."

4 Quoted in Joseph Campbell's *The Way of the Animal Powers – Historical Atlas of World Mythology.* London: Times Books, 1984.

5 See *Book of the Hopi* by Frank Waters, Ballantine edition.

6 This story is quoted and translated by Mircea Eliade in *Myth and Reality,* Harper & Row edition, 1963.

7 From Plato's *Phaedrus*, Penguin edition.

8 From Chateaubriand's *The Genius of Christianity*. Quoted in *The Oxford Book of Quotations*.

9 See Joseph Campbell's *Masks of God: Oriental Mythology* for a discussion of how Buddhism evolved after Buddha's death.

10 From Dorothy Sayer's introduction to Dante's *Divine Comedy*, Penguin edition.

11 Discussed in Melvin Morse's *Closer to the Light*. (See Bibliography.)

CHAPTER 2

1 From Plato's *The Last Days of Socrates*, Penguin edition.

2 Ian Stevenson has published several volumes of his research, listed in the bibliography.

3 From Whitton and Fisher, *Life Between Life*. (See Bibliography.)

CHAPTER 3

1 Quoted in *Is There Life After Death?* by Kastenbaum. (See Bibliography.)

2 From Plato's *Phaedrus*.

3 For documentation of this and many other equally entertaining tales, see *True Ghost Stories* by Vivienne Rae-Ellis.

CHAPTER 4

1 Raymond Moody, *Life After Life*, p. 41-42

2 Ibid. p. 44

3 Ibid. p. 45

4 Ibid. pp. 51-52

5 Ibid. p. 52

6 Ibid. p. 74

7 Melvin Morse, *Closer to the Light*.

8 Raymond Moody. Op. cit. p. 62

9 Ibid. p. 77

10 Kenneth Ring, *Heading Toward Omega*. p. 57

11 Ibid. p. 55

12 Ibid. pp. 55-56

13 From *Vital Signs* magazine, December, 1981. Quoted in *Otherworld Journeys* by Carol Zaleski.

14 Raymond Moody. Op cit. p. 62

15 Kenneth Ring. Op. cit. p. 60

16 Ibid. p. 62

17 Ibid. p. 75

18 Ibid. p. 74

19 Melvin Morse, *Transformed by the Light*. p. 17

20 Kenneth Ring. Op. cit. p. 62-63

21 Ibid. p. 70

22 Ibid. p. 68-69

23 Ibid. p. 71

24 Ibid. p. 58

25 Raymond Moody. Op. cit. p. 65-67

26 Kenneth Ring. Op. cit. p. 108

27 Robert Kastenbaum, *Is There Life After Death?*

28 Melvin Morse. *Closer to the Light*. p. 140-141

29 Melvin Morse. *Transformed by the Light*. p. 52-53

30 Margot Grey, *Return from Death*.

31 Melvin Morse. *Transformed by the Light*.

32 Ibid.

33 Ibid.

34 Ring. Op. cit. p. 98

35 Ibid. p. 96-97

CHAPTER 5

1 Frances M.M. Comper, ed. *The Book of the Craft of Dying and Other Early English Tracts Concerning Death*. London: 1917; New York: 1977. Quoted in *Otherworld Journeys* by Zaleski.

2 Adapted from a story told by Osho.

3 Osho, in *And Now, And Here*

4 From the Shambala edition of *The Tibetan Book of the Dead*.

5 Osho, in *Vigyan Bhairav Tantra*.

6 Muldoon & Carrington in *The Phenomena of Astral Projection*. For other astral travel guidance see *Far Journeys* and *Journeys Out of the Body* by Robert Monroe, and Susan Blackmore's book *Beyond the Body*, listed in the Bibliography.

7 Osho, in *Meditation: The First and Last Freedom*.

8 Proceedings of October, 1982 conference of the International Association of Near Death Studies.

9 *Vital Signs* (publication of the International Association of Near Death Studies) December, 1981.

BIBLIOGRAPHY

Albery, Nicholas, Gil Elliot, and Joseph Elliot, eds.
The Natural Death Handbook.
London: Virgin Books, 1993.

Dante Alighieri. *The Divine Comedy: Paradiso, Purgatorio, Inferno.* Translated by Dorothy Leigh Sayers.
London: Penguin Books,1949.

Bache, Christopher M. *Life Cycles: Reincarnation and the Web of Life.*
New York: Paragon House, 1991.

Barrett, W.F. *Death-Bed Visions.*
London: Methuen, 1926.

Blackmore, Susan H. *Beyond the Body: An Investigation of Out-of-the-Body Experiences.* London: William Heinemann Ltd., 1982.

Cockell, Jenny. *Yesterday's Children.*
London: Piatkus Books, 1993.

Duda, Deborah.
Coming Home – A Guide to Dying at Home with Dignity.
Santa Fe: Aurora Press, 1987.

Enright, D.J., ed. *The Oxford Book of Death.* Oxford and New York: Oxford University Press, 1983.

Gallup, George, Jr.
Adventures in Immortality.
New York: McGraw-Hill, Inc., 1982.

Grey, Margot. *Return from Death.*
London: Arkana, 1985.

Greyson, Bruce and Charles P. Flynn, eds. *The Near Death Experience – Problems, Prospects, Perspectives.* Springfield, Illinois: Charles C. Thomas, 1984.

Grof, Stanislav and Joan Halifax.
The Human Encounter with Death.
New York: Dutton, 1977.

Gurney, E., F.W.H. Myers, and F. Podmore. *Phantasms of the Living.*
2 vols. London: Trubner, 1886.
(Reprinted by Arno Press, New York: 1975)

Head, Joseph and S.L. Cranston, eds. *Reincarnation: An East-West Anthology.* Wheaton, Illinois: The Theosophical Publishing House, Quest Books, 1990.

Heinberg, Richard. *Memories & Visions of Paradise: Exploring the Universal Myth of a Lost Golden Age.* Los Angeles: Jeremy P. Tarcher, Inc., 1989; London: The Aquarian Press, 1990.

Hill, Douglas and Pat Williams.
The Supernatural.
London: Bloomsbury Books, 1989.

Humprhy, Derek. *Final Exit: The Practicalities of Self-Deliverance & Assisted Suicide for the Dying.* New York: Dell Publishing, 1991

Iverson, Jeffrey. *In Search of the Dead – A Scientific Investigation of Evidence for Life After Death.* San Francisco: HarperSanFrancisco, 1992.

Kamath, M.V. *Philosophy of Death and Dying.* Honesdale, Pennsylvania: Himalayan International Institute of Yoga, 1978.

Kastenbaum, Robert. *Is There Life After Death?* London: Rider & Co., 1984.

Maxwell, Meg and Tschudin Maxwell, eds. *Seeing the Invisible.* London: Arkana, 1990.

MacKenzie, Andrew. *Hauntings and Apparitions.* London: William Heinemann Ltd., 1982.

Moody, Raymond A., Jr. *Life After Life.* St. Simons Island, Georgia: Mockingbird Books, 1975

———. *Reflections on Life After Life.* St. Simons Island, Georgia: Mockingbird Books, 1977.

——— with Paul Perry. *The Light Beyond.* London: Macmillan, 1988; New York: Bantam Books, 1988.

———. *Life Before Life – Regression into Past Lives.* London: MacMillan, 1990.

Morse, Dr. Melvin with Paul Perry. *Closer to the Light: Learning from the Near-Death Experiences of Children.* New York: Bantam Books, 1993.

———. *Transformed by the Light: The Powerful Effect of Near-Death Experiences on People's Lives.* New York: Villard Books, 1993.

Muldoon, Sylvan and Hereward Carrington. *The Phenomena of Astral Projection.* London: Rider & Company, 1984.

Netherton, Morris, Nancy Shiffrin, and Jack Viertel. *Past Lives Therapy.* New York: William Morrow & Co., 1978.

Osho. *The Open Door.* Poona, India: Rajneesh Foundation International, 1978.

———. *And Now, And Here.* Vol. 2. Cologne, Germany: Rebel Publishing House, GmbH,: 1984.

———. *Sermons in Stones.* Cologne, Germany: Rebel Publishing House, GmbH, 1987.

———. *Meditation: The First and Last Freedom.* Cologne, Germany: Rebel Publishing House, GmbH, 1988.

———. *Vigyan Bhairav Tantra.* Cologne, Germany: Rebel Publishing House, GmbH, 1990.

Osis, Karlis and Erlendur Haraldsoon. *At the Hour of Death.* New York: Avon, 1977.

Plato. *The Republic.* Translated by Desmond Lee. London and New York: Penguin Books, Ltd., 1987.

Podmore, F. *Modern Spiritualism: A History and a Criticism.* 2 vols. London: Methuen, 1902. (Reprinted as *Mediums of the 19th Century.* Secaucus, New Jersey: University Books, 1963.)

Rae-Ellis, Vivienne, ed. *True Ghost Stories.* London: Faber & Faber, 1990.

Ring, Kenneth. *Heading Toward Omega.* New York: William Morrow, New York: 1985.

———. *Life at Death.* New York: Coward, McCann & Geoghegan, 1980.

Rinpochay, Lati and Jeffrey Hopkins. *Death, Intermediate State and Rebirth.* London: Rider & Co., 1979.

Rogo, D. Scott. *The Return from Silence: A Study of Near-Death Experiences.* London: The Aquarian Press, 1989.

Sabom, Michael. *Recollections of Death.* New York: Harper & Row, 1982.

Stevenson, Ian. *Cases of the Reincarnation Type.* Charlottesville: University Press of Virginia, 1975.

The Tibetan Book of the Dead. Translated with commentary by Francesca Fremantle and Chogyam Trungpa. Boston and London: Shambhala, 1992.

The Upanishads. Translated by Eknath Easwaran. London and New York: Arkana, 1988.

Virgil. *The Aeneid.* Translated by C. Day Lewis. Oxford: Oxford University Press, 1991.

Whitton, Joel and Joe Fisher. *Life Between Life.* New York: Doubleday, 1986.

Woolger, Roger J. *Other Lives, Other Selves.* London: The Aquarian Press, 1990; and New York: Dolphin/Doubleday, 1987.

Zaleski, Carol. *Otherworld Journeys: Accounts of Near-Death Experience in Medieval and Modern Times.* Oxford and New York: Oxford University Press, 1987.

PHOTOS ACKNOWLEDGMENTS

CARMEN STRIDER, 1, 143, 170, 174; **TATE GALLERY**, London, 2/3, 18; **PREMGIT**, Devon, 5, 80, 179, 181, 212, 216/217; **BRIDGEMAN ART LIBRARY**, London, 6/7, 11, 17, 22, 26/27, 30, 38, 46/47, 55, 58/59, 66, 67, 70, 74, 76, 77, 78/79, 86, 87, 90, 95, 106/107, 118, 123, 134/135, 145, 147, 148, 162, 194/195, 206, 210/211, 215, 220, 222; **COURTAULD INSTITUTE OF ART**, London, 13; **SCALA**, Firenze, 14, 192; **WERNER FORMAN ARCHIVE**, London, 23, 75, 99, 186, 200; **MARY EVANS PICTURE LIBRARY**, London, 25, 28/29, 32/33, 37, 41, 44/45, 48, 49, 50, 51, 52/53, 56/57, 60/61, 62, 64, 65, 68/69, 71, 72/73, 84, 88, 89, 91, 92/93, 100, 101, 109, 111, 112, 113, 116/117, 120/121, 122, 125, 130/131, 132/133, 138, 140/141, 149, 151, 153, 154, 157, 172, 218; **TYNE AND WEAR MUSEUMS**, Newcastle, 34/35; **BODLEIAN LIBRARY**, Oxford, 39; **ROBIN RICHMOND**, London, 42; **NATIONAL MUSEUM OF THE AMERICAN INDIAN**, 63; **SIDD MURRAY-CLARK**, 82, 167; **SIMON MARSDEN**, Lincoln, 105, 161, 169, 205; **FORTEAN PICTURE LIBRARY**, Clwyd, 108, 114, 142; **ROGER MITCHELL**, Gwent, 119; **MUSÉE DU LOUVRE**, Paris, 127; **THE COLLEGE OF PSYCHIC STUDIES**, London, 159; **OSHO INTERNATIONAL FOUNDATION**, Swami Prem Siddhena, 165, 190, 198, 201, 208; **DOVER PUBLICATIONS**, New York, 173; **KOMALA JACQUIER**, Genève, 182/183, 214; **BOYAN BRECELJ**, 184; **SCIENCE PHOTO LIBRARY**, London, 203.

TEXT ACKNOWLEDGMENTS

TRANSFORMED BY THE LIGHT by Melvin L. Morse and Paul Perry, © 1992 by Melvin L. Morse and Paul Perry, reprinted by permission of Villard Books, a division of Random House, Inc.: 157, 166, 168-169, 170-171, 172-173, 175; **THE TIBETAN BOOK OF THE DEAD** translated with commentary by Francesca Fremantle and Chögyam Trungpa, © 1975 by Francesca Fremantle and Chögyam Trungpa, reprinted by arrangement with Shambhala Publications, Inc., 300 Massachusetts Avenue, Boston, MA 02115: 87, 192-193; **LIFE AFTER LIFE** by Raymond A. Moody, Jr., reprinted by permission of Mockingbird Books, St. Simon's Island, Georgia: 122, 128, 129, 136, 137-138, 140, 143, 144, 145, 150-151, 155, 164; **IS THERE LIFE AFTER DEATH?** by Robert Kastenbaum, reprinted by permission of Multimedia Books Ltd.: 166; **RETURN FROM DEATH** by Margot Grey (Arkana, 1985), © Margot Grey, 1985: 168-169; **THE UPANISHADS**, translated by Eknath Easwaran (Arkana, 1988), © The Blue Mountain Center of Meditation, 1987: 87, 104, 152; **THE NATURAL DEATH HANDBOOK** edited by Nicholas Albery, Gil Elliot, and Joseph Elliot, reprinted by permission of Virgin Publishing Ltd.: 209, 216; **WILDFIRE MAGAZINE**, P.O. Box 9167, Spokane, WA 99209-9167, USA: 24; **WISDOM OF THE SANDS** by Osho, Volume 1, © Osho International Foundation, published by Rebel Publishing House, GmbH. 1980: 83; **SERMONS IN STONES** by Osho, © Osho International Foundation, published by Rebel Publishing House, GmbH. 1987: 140; **VIGYAN BHAIRAV TANTRA** by Osho, © Osho International Foundation, published by Rebel Publishing House, GmbH. 1990: 196-197; **MEDITATION: THE FIRST AND LAST FREEDOM** by Osho, © Osho International Foundation, published by Rebel Publishing House, GmbH. 1988: 205; **THIS IS IT** by Alan W. Watts, reproduced by permission of Random House, Inc. New York: 36; **DIVINE COMEDY, PARADISO, PURGATORIO, INFERNO** by Dante, from Dorothy L. Sayer's introduction, Penguin edition, reproduced by permission of David Higham Associates, London: 71-72; **AT THE HOUR OF DEATH** by Karlis Osis and Erlendur Haraldsson, 1977, reprinted by permission of Avon Books, New York: 124, 128-129; **HEADING TOWARD OMEGA** by Kenneth Ring, 1985, reproduced by permission of William Morrow, New York: 150, 152, 155, 156-157, 158, 160, 163, 164, 176-177, 178; **CLOSER TO THE LIGHT: LEARNING FROM THE NEAR-DEATH EXPERIENCES OF CHILDREN** by Melvin Morse with Paul Perry, 1990, reproduced by permission of Bantam Books, New York: 77, 130-131, 149, 167-168; **LIFE BEFORE LIFE: REGRESSION INTO PAST LIVES** by Raymond Moody, 1990, reproduced by permission of Bantam Books, New York: 102-103; **MEMORIES AND VISIONS OF PARADISE: EXPLORING THE UNIVERSAL MYTH OF A LOST GOLDEN AGE** by Richard Heinberg, 1989, reproduced by permission of Jeremy P. Tarcher, Inc., Los Angeles: 40, 48, 146; **OTHERWORLD JOURNEYS: ACCOUNTS OF NEAR-DEATH EXPERIENCE IN MEDIEVAL AND MODERN TIMES** by Carol Zaleski, 1987, reproduced by permission of Oxford University Press, New York: 155, 184.

Every effort has been made to trace all present copyright holders of the material used in this book, whether companies or individuals. Any omission is unintentional and we will be pleased to correct any errors in future editions of this book.